CAMEOS THAT COUNTED

RITCHIE
CHARACTER
STUDY
SERIES

CAMEOS THAT COUNTED

VOLUME 1

INFLUENTIAL CHARACTERS RARELY MENTIONED IN THE BIBLE

A. J. HIGGINS

RITCHIE
John Ritchie Publishing

40 Beansburn, Kilmarnock, Scotland

ISBN-13: 978 1 914273 45 2

Copyright © 2023 by John Ritchie Ltd.
40 Beansburn, Kilmarnock, Scotland

www.ritchiechristianmedia.co.uk

Typeset by John Ritchie Ltd., Kilmarnock
Printed by Bell & Bain Ltd., Glasgow.

ABOUT THE AUTHOR

A. J. Higgins MD was saved in 1965 and has been associated with the believers who gather to the Lord's Name in Barrington N.J. He is married to his wife Ruth, and they had two daughters, one of which went home to be with the Lord in 2021, and two grandchildren. He was a practicing physician for over 45 years. He has served in fellowship with his brethren in the leadership of the local assembly and moves among Scripturally gathered assemblies ministering the Word of God.

He has been editor of *Truth and Tidings* for twenty years and has authored several books: *Proverbs*, in the WTBT series, a work on *Marriage and the Family*, and a volume on *Samuel, Prophet and Kingmaker*, in the current series of works.

Contents

Foreword

We do not know who wrote the Epistle to the Hebrews but whoever it was knew the Old Testament well and was familiar with the characters whose experiences are a feature of the letter. As a result, the Holy Spirit could draw on this knowledge to ensure that the great truths God intended us to learn were fully covered. Abraham, Moses, Aaron, Joshua and Melchisedec are names found early in the book. Then one comes to chapter 11 and the list there is impressive and could have been longer and more detailed, "but" the author exclaims "time would fail me to tell". Some of these characters are given much space in Scripture and accordingly have much to teach us, but even those who make only a brief appearance are to be noted and valued. Hebrews was written by someone who, as the human instrument, had a mind saturated with the Word of God.

In any series of character studies men such as Moses, Joseph, Jacob, and David, each afford material for a complete volume (or a series of ministry addresses). The list of major characters in Scripture is long and includes those who provide warnings as well as positive features. The Ritchie Character Study Series currently has only around 10 titles out of the many (to which the author of this book, Dr Higgins, has contributed). No doubt others will follow.

However, it is also true that we have heard or read highly profitable ministry that refers to characters about whom we know a limited amount. As noted above, Hebrews 11 reminds us of their value. Several make significant but relatively short cameo appearances in the text of Hebrews. Abel, Enoch, Rahab, and Barak are among them. Beyond Hebrews one can add individuals such as Anna, Elisabeth, and Dorcas. I have noted these women, without knowledge of whom we would have been spiritually the poorer, to emphasise that God has used both men and women to help us learn from their experience. In this volume you will find these women among others taken from both Old and New Testaments, and men who similarly make short but important contributions to the Word of God, such as Barzillai, Enoch, Nathan, and Mephibosheth.

The great doctrines of Scripture, Justification, Redemption, Sanctification among others demand careful study and are often illuminated by reference to appropriate characters. It is also true that teaching on how we ought to behave is likewise illustrated by individuals in Scripture.

It is good advice, therefore, to encourage one another in the study of Bible characters. Those characters covered here will repay time spent in meditating on their stories. We are indebted once again to Dr Higgins for his customary diligence and care. He avoids flights of fancy in the applications he makes but gives ample healthy spiritual food to instruct and enjoy. If it stimulates the reader to meditate on and develop these particular studies and also to search the Scriptures for other examples from which to learn, then this book will have proved its value.

Introduction

There are men and women who grace the pages of Scriptures who have become virtual household names to all believers, names such as Peter, Paul, James, Abraham, David, and Samuel. Their lives are portrayed over many chapters of Scripture. Some we can trace from birth through to old age. Others are presented at varied segments of their lives as they move on to the stage of Sacred history to perform their God-given function in His great story of redemption.

But there are also individuals who make cameo appearances and others whose biographies are given in a few short glimpses. Yet these are not less important in the divine story as it unfolds through the ages. Though Scripture may use an economy of words to tell of their lives, the results of their actions have been eternally inscribed in the Word of God which shall "never pass away." Cameo appearances have, at times, had copious consequences. Thus, their contributions will live on eternally for all to appreciate and from which we can all profit in the present time. Names such as Hushai, Dorcas, Barzillai, Jonathan, Simeon, and Anna reveal lives which were useful and honouring to God, even though summarised in a few verses of Holy writ.

All of this should also serve, not only as instruction for us, but also as encouragement. None of us is a David or Peter, few of us, if any, will ever know the experiences of the great heroes of the faith. None of this is a reason to feel that the contribution that you make to the work of God is insignificant. We are all minor players in the great drama of redemption. But we can thank God that we are part of His great work in this age. And, just as these seemingly lesser lights contributed in their day to the work of God, so we can as well in the day in which God has placed us.

We are Sunday School teachers, personal workers, shepherds, and servants. Some of you are among the caring who bring a dinner to a shut-in, bake a cake for a neighbour recently bereaved, or open your home to someone needing a shoulder upon which to cry, or an ear open to allow someone to unburden herself. None of this makes the magazines as news; no public commendation or recognition hails your act of kindness. But nothing is unnoticed by the eye that sees the falling sparrow that no other eye tracks.

Think of the loss to David if there had been no Hushai; of what we would be deprived of if we did not have the songs of Elisabeth, Zacharias, and Simeon. Who can measure the comfort that Onesiphorus was to Paul or the impact of the "fervent prayer" of Epaphroditus for the believers in Colosse?

As you read these brief notes on the lives of these believers, may you be encouraged in your own devotion and service to the Lord. Yes, we are all minor players, but what a drama in which we are privileged to participate! "Your labour is not in vain in the Lord" (1 Cor 15:58).

Amram and Jochebed

"There is eternal influence and power in motherhood."

Reading: *Exodus 2:1-10; Hebrews 11:23*

Their Family

Amram and Jochebed, on the surface, would not rate as very prominent figures in Scripture. Amram's name is mentioned 14 times; Jochebed, his wife, gets even fewer. Yet think of the family they raised: Aaron, Miriam, and Moses. Hands down, this is the most famous, and possibly the most important family in the Old Testament, maybe in all of history. We have several families in the New Testament which would compete for the top slot – Mary, Martha, and Lazarus; or perhaps Salome and Zebedee along with their two sons, James and John would qualify. What a privilege to be an Amram and Jochebed!

Imagine giving to the world Aaron, Miriam, and Moses! Think of the consequences of their lives upon the nation of Israel, the western world, and even eternity. Until very recently, all of Western society took its bearing and rested its foundation on the Mosaic Law. True, it did not come from Moses, but he was its vessel chosen by God to bring it to us. Wherever it was followed, stability and security followed.

The Aaronic priesthood and all it secured for the nation of Israel began with Aaron. He was allowed to represent the people before God and to oversee the sacrificial system. Miriam is one of only five women in Scripture referred to as a prophetess (Ex 15:20). She led the women in song at the Red Sea and caused worship to ascend to the throne of God. The blot on her life in Numbers 12 should not obscure the greatness of this woman and her contribution, whether we find her by the Nile watching over the babe in the ark, or by the Red Sea leading the women in song.

If nothing more were recorded of this eminent couple other than the family they raised, their contribution to the work of God on earth would still be significant. But once again the day defined the deed as they raised their family in very dark and difficult days. As such, they serve as an encouragement for present 21st century families. Each generation probably has said the same as I am about to say. There has never been a more difficult day in which to raise a family. And what each generation has said is true as conditions worsen for each succeeding family. There was the bondage of Egypt, the Nile and its crocodiles that demanded every newborn male, the taskmasters whip, and the deferment of the long-expected fulfilment of divine promises. The days were dark and tinged by a sense of hopelessness for many in Israel – but not for Amram and Jochebed.

In our age, our society, like the Nile, is demanding our children for indoctrination. The silence of heaven amidst the injustice and iniquity in our society is a "trial of faith" (1 Pet 1:7) for everyone. Egypt attempted to thwart the birth of newborn sons (Ex 1:15, 16). If unsuccessful there, then terminate their growth (1:22). If that did not prove successful, then so trouble their lives with bondage and bricks, that they would not be able to be anything for God (1:14). The strategy of the enemy is eerily similar today. What resources did Amram and Jochebed have in their day? What do we have available to us today?

Their Faith

They began their married life well. He was of the tribe of Levi and married a woman from the tribe of Levi. He married within the nation and within the tribe. Their marriage had all the earmarks of devotion to God, and we would expect smooth sailing. Yet, God gave them a son at the darkest moment of Israel's history in her bondage in Egypt. Faith was going to be tried. As the days and weeks passed, their faith was being tested and was growing.

We read in Exodus 2:2 that when Jochebed saw that he was a goodly child, she hid him three months. Every newborn child, and especially every newborn soul, represents potential for God. When Ruth bore her son Obed, the women of the city saw great potential in his life (Ruth

4:15). Similarly, we need eyes to see that every soul has potential for God to use to accomplish great things. Those small children who run around the Hall making noise between the meetings represent the future. May God give us eyes to see.

Scripture is always balanced and insightful. Notice that Exodus 2 credits Jochebed with preserving Moses' life. In Acts 7, in Stephen's great discourse, he tells us that Moses, the infant, was hidden in his father's house (Acts 7:20) because he was exceedingly "fair to God." We come next to Hebrews 11 and find that "By faith, Moses when he was born was hid three months of his parents because they saw he was a comely child" (v 23).

Now notice carefully: Exodus says that his mother hid him. Acts says that it was his father's house. Hebrews says that his parents hid him. Exodus tells us of a mother's hand that protected; Acts stress the headship of the home in Amram. Hebrews tells us that they were in harmony as to the action. Communication was essential for this couple.

Focus on the Hebrew passage for a moment. In that chapter which emphasises the importance of faith, and the covenant promises of God, it is again stressed that Moses' parents acted by faith. But faith requires a word from God upon which to base its action. Faith is never a leap in the dark or an "I hope so" attitude. What revelation did Moses' parents grasp and act on? It may be the covenant God made with Abram and the promise that after 400 years they would be delivered (Gen 15); or it might have been the prophetic-promise of Joseph in Genesis 50:24, 25, recounting that God would visit them and bring them up out of Egypt. Is it possible that as they looked at the newborn babe, they thought that here might be the deliverer who would lead the people of God out of Egypt? Or did they simply see a child that had potential for God and refused to allow Egypt to have him? Whichever scenario was operative, they obviously knew the Word of God that was handed down orally from generation to generation.

Add to this that his mother made an ark to save him in the Nile, likely taking her cue from Noah and his ark that saved his family from the flood waters, and we see a family that was steeped in the knowledge of God's ways. There was no written Scripture to which they could turn, but there was the oral tradition of divine promises and dealings to which they could resort for their faith. We who have the completed canon have so much more upon which to build our lives and shape our decisions, yet we come so far short of what some of these O. T. believers displayed.

Their Fearlessness

"They were not afraid of the king's commandment" (11:23). They did not fear man, but they did move in the fear of God, that longing desire to please Him alone. As we trace their follow-through and strategy, we see their wisdom based on the experience of previous believers, their care for detail, and their confidence in God.

Had the Lord given them another daughter instead of a son, life would have been much easier. But the Lord had other purposes. He was working, not only to produce a Moses, but to increase the faith and joy of Amram and Jochebed. So, He gave them a son and put their faith to the test.

The main "hands-on" of raising children is entrusted to a mother. True to form, Jochebed seems to occupy the spotlight in all that follows with Moses. The king's command demanded he be thrown into the Nile. The potential of the child for God demanded a different course to Jochebed. Initially, she protected and hid him from the eyes of everyone. For three months she somehow kept him secreted from the Egyptian Gestapo. In a similar manner, Christian mothers will "hide" their children and shield them from the secular world and its standards for as long as possible. But a time came when Moses could no longer be hid. She had protected him as long as possible and now she must see him preserved in the Nile. As mentioned, she duplicated Noah's ark on a smaller scale, pitching it with pitch to keep the Nile out. When she could no longer hide him she could hedge him about to preserve him. Although he had to be in the Nile, she could do what was needed to keep the Nile from being in his ark.

The events that ensued are well known and declare eloquently the sovereignty of God. He uses the tear from the babe, a whimper, combined with the sympathy of a woman's heart. And the result is that the conqueror of Egypt is brought into the house of Pharaoh to be raised as Pharaoh's son. God oversaw the perfect timing of everything: the ark in the right place, Pharaoh's daughter arriving on the scene at the proper moment, Miriam's arrival, the agreement to have a Hebrew "nurse" care for the child. The results include the irony of a mother being paid to care for her own child! The years spent back at home with Jochebed would be years that would be put to good use. It was during that time that his mother would have instructed him in the promises and purposes of God. What she instilled into his heart is what enabled him to make the right choice later in life. She had protected him from Egypt as long as she could. Then she preserved him with the ark. But now she prepared him for the service God had in mind for him.

Early years of development are crucial for the preparation of our children should God in mercy save them. Increasingly, a secular society is demanding that we hand our children over to their educational system and allow it to shape their minds, values, and vision. It wants to "drown" them, immerse them in its river of secularism and humanistic thinking. Parents have the responsibility to prepare a child for God and His service. This can only be accomplished by giving the Word of God its place in the family. With the intrusion of all of our "devices," this has become increasingly difficult.

We are told in Hebrews that Amram and Jochebed had to wait until Moses came to years to see the ultimate choice he would make. Putting Scriptures together, we find that it was at the age of 40 that Moses made the choice to cast his lot in with the children of Israel. Godly parents who raised their son for God had to wait forty years to be sure he would make the right decision in life and link himself with the future Messiah. The same patience is needed for many parents today. You may have raised your child with the desire to see him or her useful for God. Years have passed and you still pray, sometimes with tears, that God will work in that life. Take heart and remember these parents and their patient waiting on God. And think of the result – a Moses!

Ananias

He knew "how to speak a word in season to him that is weary"

Isaiah 50:4

Reading: *Acts 9:10-19; 22:12-16*

Ananias is introduced to us in Acts 9:10-18, and is again referred to by Paul in his defense before the rioting crowd in Acts 22:12-16. Ananias makes a brief appearance in the sacred history and then fades into the background, the remainder of his life known only to God. We should not assume that there was nothing else of significance in his life. But there may not have been anything so significant as the brief visit he paid to "brother Saul" on that memorable day.

We are again reminded that God may use obscure saints to accomplish crucial tasks that have major consequences for the work of the kingdom of God. Ananias was privy to the fact that God had great things in store for the new convert, Saul, and with no sense of jealousy or resentment, he carried out his responsibility to him. It should be an encouragement to all of us that the Lord may direct us to some seemingly small task. But in the doing of it, we are setting in motion events that may well have monumental consequences. Ours is the responsibility of listening and obeying when He directs.

Gathering up the fourteen verses which tell us of him, there are some insightful lessons to be gleaned for our profit.

His Testimony

When Paul gave his defence before the chief captain, the soldiers, and the temple mob, he alluded to Ananias, characterising him as a "a devout man according to the law, having a good report of all the

Jews which dwelt there (Damascus)" (22:12). For obvious reasons, Paul would introduce the fact that it was a devout man with a good testimony among the Jews in the city who had identified with him after his Damascus Road experience. But the value of his testimony should not be lost on us.

God was looking for a man to bring his message to the new convert, Saul of Tarsus. He had just such a man positioned right there in Damascus. Here was the kind of man that God could employ.

Psalm 24 attests to the truth that those moving in fellowship with God are men and women who have clean hands, a pure heart, humble souls, and truthful lips. God can use a Balaam and a Caiaphas when He so chooses. But they are the exceptions worked by His sovereignty. He normally delights to use believers who are walking in fellowship with Him. Ananias was such a man.

Is my life and testimony such that the Lord can use me? If I need to make changes in my life if God should call, then I am not a clean vessel "meet for the Master's use."

His Availability

He is introduced in Acts 9:10 as "a certain disciple," a designation only used three times in the book of Acts. His words, "Behold I am here Lord," show us a man who was in touch with heaven. The call did not "interrupt" his life or come as a huge surprise. It seems as though it was almost natural for him to be in communication with heaven.

God had to call but once and Ananias could say, "Behold, I am here Lord" (Acts 9:10). Others responded in a similar manner and were useful for the Lord. Isaiah's, "Here am I. Send me" (Isa 6:8), and Samuel's thrice delayed, "speak for Thy servant heareth" (1 Sam 3:10) have become the standard for all believers.

Instructions were given to Ananias concerning a new convert. He would be found praying. God had revealed a similar balancing truth to Saul. He had prepared Saul and now was preparing Ananias. But Ananias at first had some reservations. He had a deep concern for the believers in Damascus. He had heard of Saul's persecution of the believers in Jerusalem and knew of his authority to carry out the same in Damascus. Concerned for the well-being of the saints, he had his fears. God's assurance, however, enabled him to overcome and obey.

Ananias had natural fears, national concerns, and spiritual reasons for hesitating. But the reassurance from the Lord caused him to obey. At that point in time, his obedience was immediate. His task was to bring assurance and focus to a new convert. One of the first things he would do would be to teach Saul the need for baptism.

His Spirit of Forgiveness

Ananias not only obeyed the Lord and went to Saul, but his first words to him were, "Brother Saul." Ananias was speaking to a man who was responsible for harming many believers and hounding many to death. Here he was facing an enemy of God's people, the one-man Gestapo from the Israeli "anti-Christian police." How was he going to act? What would he say? As soon as he enters the room, his first words must have fallen with incredible sweetness on Saul's ears: "Brother Saul." With two words, Ananias conveyed the forgiveness of his heart and a welcome to the community of believers.

The revelation of the mystery of the "One Body" was revealed to Paul at a later date. It characterised Paul's ministry throughout his service for the Lord. But those initial words, suggesting a oneness together in the family of God, were a precious introduction to that truth.

Forbearing and forgiving are commanded of us all (Col 3:13). Forgiveness is a nice concept. The problem is when you really have something to forgive, we all make excuses, covered over with spiritual veneer to soothe our consciences. But we are slow to forgive. Ananias did it immediately. Nothing less is expected of us.

His Sensitivity

Ananias was a man who knew how to speak a word in season. What he said and how he said it are important. It is a reminder to us all that words are important. They are important for their meaning, but also for the time when they are said, and the manner in which they are said. Many things that Job's friends said were statements of truth. The problem was that they were not relevant to Job. Their diatribes on retribution theology were totally "out of season" for Job.

Sensitivity for the burdens and cares of other believers is a skill which many of us sadly lack. So often our comments are cold and cutting. There are the single believers among us who are made to feel "incomplete" by our innuendos. There are the grieving parents who long for the salvation of their children, and instead of encouragement from us, they feel judged by us, as though their failure has led to the rebellion of their children. There are heavy hearts, lonely hearts, and sorrowing hearts that are longing for someone to reach out and communicate something of the tenderness and sympathy of God. Sadly, we disappoint them by our inability. The Perfect Servant, though no less than God incarnate, chose to begin His day in communion with God. Flowing out from those times of nearness sprang the ability, as a Servant, to know how to speak a word in season to the weary. More time spent in the presence of God might enable us also to have words that would be seasonable for the people of God.

His Encouragement

In Acts 22, Paul affords us additional details about that initial visit from Ananias. Along with teaching the need for baptism, the words of Ananias as recorded in Acts 22, tell us of how wisely Ananias dealt with Saul. The experience on the Damascus road was life-changing and overwhelming. No doubt, the new convert was filled with questions and uncertainties. Ananias linked his new found faith all the way back to "The God of our fathers" confirming that the Messiah long looked for was the Christ he had seen on the road. Importantly, Ananias gave Saul a sense of direction and purpose for his Christian life. He was going to be a witness unto all men. The Lord had told him prior to going to Saul's side, that Saul was a chosen vessel to bear His name before the Gentiles, kings, and the children of Israel. Ananias wisely gave Paul a sense of purpose for his life for God.

Shepherds and parents alike can be a great blessing to young believers by teaching baptism and also the fact that all are saved for a purpose, for some work to do for the Lord. The young believer needs wise shepherd care, a care that includes encouragement and the instilling of a vision for usefulness in the assembly and beyond.

Andrew

"All God's giants have been weak men who did great things for God because they reckoned on God being with them."

J Hudson Taylor

Reading: *Mark 1:16-18; John 1:35-42; John 6:1-13*

A Little Man and a Big Move

Andrew does not occupy the same prominence in the gospel records as do Peter and John, or even James for that matter. Someone has likened him to Benaiah in the O. T., one of David's mighty men who did not make it into the "top three" (2 Sam 3:23). He is mentioned on perhaps four occasions outside of the times when his name is listed as one of the disciples. In the estimation of men, he would be considered a "lesser" disciple, one who did not occupy the limelight to any degree. He preached no memorable sermons, encountered no great crisis, and has not left us any writings from which we can learn. There are, however, lessons from his life from which we can all profit.

At some point in time, Andrew made his way from Bethsaida to the Jordan to link himself with the Baptist through baptism. He made a move away from the nation and submitted to the baptism of repentance. He became known as one of John's disciples (John 1:35, 40).

But there came a day when he stood by as John pointed out "the Lamb of God". Andrew and John left the Baptist and began following this "Lamb." When the Lord asked the memorable question, "What seekest thou?" they were quick to respond, "Master, where dwellest Thou?" Andrew now made another significant move as he followed the Messiah, the Christ. The remainder of that day and night were spent with the Lord, learning of Him.

Sometime later, by the Sea of Galilee, Andrew was working on the fishing nets with his brother Peter and his father (Mark 1:16, 17), when a call came. It was a call from the Lord Jesus, a call to discipleship. "Come ye after Me and I will make you to become fishers of men" (Mark 1:17). His response was immediate. All was left and another move was made, a very big one, this time leaving all behind to follow the Lord Jesus.

Your life and mine may not have the dramatic encounters that Andrew's knew, but we all have been directed first to the Lamb of God as our sin-bearer and Saviour, and then to the Lord Who commands and deserves our obedient following. Some will quibble that the word "disciple" is not mentioned after the book of Acts and that somehow it is not a relevant subject for today. And while I must concede that the word is absent in the epistles, the demands of discipleship as given by the Lord Jesus are all present in the epistles: forsake, follow, take up the cross, and learn.

Andrew's response to the call was immediate. Ours should not be any less so. The One Who called Andrew continues to call us to faithful following and service.

A Little Man and a Big Man

Andrew's first reaction to having found the Messiah was to rush home and tell his brother Peter. His testimony was simple but marked by clarity. "We have found the Messiah ... the Christ" (John 1:41). It appears that those few words were the totality of his testimony. Perhaps it was breathless excitement, or maybe he was trying to whet the appetite of a brother whom he knew was waiting, as was he, for the Messiah. Whatever the case, his testimony was effective in that it led Peter to his own encounter with Christ (John 1:42).

It would be later that the Lord promised to make Andrew a "fisher of men," but Andrew had already caught his biggest fish. Andrew would not be the one to stand forth on the day of Pentecost and preach to over 3,000 souls. He would not be the one who would enter into the standing-room-only crowd in Cornelius' home and present the gospel (Acts 10). The crowds and the big events were for Peter and not Andrew. But Andrew had been the one who had brought Peter to Christ.

It was a shoemaker who was preaching and whom God used to reach C. H. Spurgeon as a young boy of 15, on a snowy Sunday morning. It was a Sunday School teacher, Edward Kimball, who spoke to D. L. Moody, leading to his conversion. Did you ever hear of Edward Kimball? Hugh Latimer was reached through a man named Thomas Bilney, a man they referred to as "Little Bilney." Many a very useful evangelist was saved through the "preaching" of his mother. God uses whom He chooses to reach those who will be prominent in the public aspect of His work.

When Andrew brought his brother to Christ, he was fulfilling the work God had for him. When Peter stood before the crowd on Pentecost Day, he was likewise carrying out what God had for him. That is all we are each responsible to do.

A Little Man and a Great Miracle

It was a memorable day, not soon forgotten by all who were there. The crowd had followed the Lord, listening to His teaching. Many were healed as a result of the compassion and care of the Shepherd. As the day began to end, the Lord addressed Philip about the need. Philip looked at the size of the crowd and doubted that they had resources sufficient to meet the need. Andrew had come in contact with a lad with five loaves and two fish. But he doubted the adequacy of the supply. Philip was overwhelmed by the need; Andrew by the meagerness of the resources. Both doubted the sufficiency of their Lord.

But Andrew did bring the boy to Christ. In the hands of the Lord Jesus, the need was met as He divided and kept dividing until all were filled.

Andrew's actions would lead to a meal and a message. The sermon on the Bread of Life has fed far more down through the centuries than the supply of the loaves and fishes. But the material supply was what enabled the Lord to teach of the spiritual supply. Those who saw only the material need being met, were intent on making Christ their King (John 6:14). All who have, through the years, understood the spiritual import of the message have hastened to make Him their Lord.

It has probably not been lost on the reader that Andrew who brought his brother to Christ, now brought a boy to Christ. His versatility in wining souls is to be emulated. Andrew shines as a personal worker. Not everyone is able to preach publicly; some are gifted to speak personally to souls, winning them to the Lord.

A Little Man and a Future Mission

The Lord left Bethany and the supper that Martha had prepared for Him. Then, the Lord Jesus entered Jerusalem on that last week of His earthly sojourn, riding on the colt. The city hailed Him even though they would soon reject Him. The crowds went before and followed. Hosannas echoes through the streets of the Old City. Among those who were present were certain Gentiles, Greeks, who had come up to Passover. They approached Philip, perhaps out of curiosity, requesting an audience with the Lord Jesus. Philip, not knowing what to do, searched out Andrew. Then together they approached the Lord. Andrew was there when the Lord had looked on the Samaritans coming to see Him and had heard the Lord say, "Look on the fields." He was there when the Lord had said, "other sheep I have, which are not of this fold: them also I must bring, and they shall hear my voice; and there shall be one fold, and one shepherd" (John 10:16). He knew of the Lord's interest in Gentiles and of the ultimate purpose to include them in blessing. The full scope of that, the mystery revealed to Paul, was still a "secret" in the heart of God. But he knew His Saviour's heart of compassion.

As a result of Andrew's actions, the Lord revealed once more the truth of His death and its fruitfulness. The events that followed included the statement concerning His soul being troubled, the voice from heaven, the promise that He would draw all men, including those Greeks, unto Him (John 12:32), and the final words of the Christ to the nation (John 12:49, 40).

Little did Andrew realise that the great work of world-wide evangelism, a gospel that would embrace both Jew and Gentile, would one day be heralded. But in bringing the Greeks to Christ, he was anticipating that future day.

A Little Man and a Faithful Martyr

Bible dictionaries and commentaries differ on the location of Andrew's death. All seem united that he died a martyr, faithful to His Lord. Some place him in southern Russia, stoned to death for his faith. Other locate his end in Greece or in Asia Minor. The majority have him martyred in Patras. The important thing is that he was faithful in his testimony and sealed it with his life.

So, in the end, Andrew was not really a "little man." Any man or woman who finishes the course God has designed for him or her, and who fulfils the purpose and will of God for his life, is really a Man in Christ, fully grown up and mature, as "big" as God can make a person! God did not make many Peters; but we can each be an Andrew!

Anna

"I have learned in whatsoever state I am, therewith to be content ... I can do all things through Christ which strengtheneth me"

Apostle Paul

Reading: *Luke 2:22-38*

Luke's gospel record is marked by a literary device that results in a very readable and engaging account. Among his techniques, Luke often links two people together throughout his record. At times, the individuals contrast, the one with the other. Take for example the two sons in Luke 15, or the two thieves on the cross, the rich man and Lazarus in Luke 16, or the two debtors of chapter 7. In other instances, the two individuals complement each other. His gospel opens with several pairs of believers seen as part of a godly remnant. There are Zacharias and Elisabeth, Joseph and Mary, and Simeon and Anna. He closes with two on the road to Emmaus. Although Simeon and Anna complement each other, there are significant differences that we will discover as we trace her life and experience.

It is noteworthy that Luke is considered by all to be the gospel written to Gentiles, to the Grecian world. Yet it is in this "Gentile gospel" that we are introduced to a faithful Jewish remnant awaiting the coming Messiah. This contrasts with Matthew, the "Jewish gospel," where we see Gentiles coming to find the King (Matt 2), amidst the seeming indifference of the leaders of the nation (Matt 1).

Her Widowhood

Without making too much of names, Anna's name (a Greek form of Hannah), means "gracious." She was from the tribe of Asher, or "happy." This much can be said about Anna regardless of how much we might spiritualise names, she lived up her to name. She was a gracious and contented woman.

Life had been difficult for her. Commentators disagree over whether she was 84 years old or a widow for 84 years. Either condition would represent a significant trial for any saint of God. She had enjoyed a brief seven years of married life. Then, likely very unexpectedly, her husband was taken from her. Widowhood in first century life, was a very lonely and difficult path. It meant monetary and social loss. There were no welfare systems to help nor social programs to assist widows. She was alone.

How did she respond to her circumstances? Couple the events in her personal life with the condition of the nation. History tells us that, subsequent to the Maccabees and their revolts, the office of High priest was up for sale. It was no longer a direct descendant of Aaron who wore the golden mitre. Also, the Pharisees were infamous for defrauding widows of their homes. The nation as a whole was away from God. The Scribes had little interest in the worship of the true God. Everyone had vested interests in maintaining the status quo. The temple itself had become a place for monetary gain, symptomatic of the spiritual condition of the nation. Conditions were rife for a godly widow to become bitter and to isolate herself in her cocoon of self-pity and self-righteous anger. Yet we read that in her widowhood, she chose to use her time for the Lord.

She joins an illustrious list of God's octogenarians who lived for God at an age when most believers assume a cruise-control Christianity. Think of Caleb, Moses, Barzillai, Abram and Sarah, to name a few.

Hers was a simple life, marked by self-denial and spiritual exercise.

It is comparatively easy to justify our lack of spiritual commitment by referring to the hypocrisy of others, the lack of great preachers amongst us, and the general condition of spiritual malaise in the land today. Then there is the natural tendency with aging to feel that we have arrived! Anna tolerated none of these thoughts. She was living for God despite the spiritual state of the nation and her own circumstances. Aging brings with it the danger of self-complacency. We must avoid at all costs a past-tense Christianity!

Her Worship

Simeon came by the Spirit into the temple. But Anna departed not from the temple. She was in the right place at the right time to look upon the right object of worship. Luke's gospel is filled with temple scenes. In each we learn new and valuable lessons. It was here, in the House of God, that she received a fresh appreciation of Christ. We should be occupied with Christ daily in our private mediations on Him. But there should as well be a freshness when we gather in "House of God" in our grasp of the Lord Jesus.

As we listen to Simeon and his thanksgiving (Luke 2:29-31), it is evident that he has a cosmic view of the coming of Christ: the nations as well as Israel, time as well as eternity will be touched by the advent of this child. But Anna, in contrast, had a more personal view. Her circumstances, widowhood, would have made her keenly aware of the law of the Kinsman Redeemer. Widowhood had prepared her to value and to look for a Kinsman Redeemer. Note that she gave thanks to God and spoke about this child to all that were looking for redemption in Israel. We can leave aside for a moment the question as to whether it was redemption from Rome or the much more important spiritual redemption. Her appreciation of Christ was framed by her circumstances.

God had allowed circumstances into her life to afford her an appreciation of Christ distinct from Simeon's, the Magi of Matthew 1, and even the shepherds mentioned earlier in the chapter. We learn from this that one of the purposes of trial is to prepare us to appreciate the Lord Jesus in fresh ways. I doubt that Anna chafed at her widowhood once she saw Christ. Likewise, none of us will look back from eternity to some of earth's trials with regret if they have revealed the Lord to us in a fresh manner. In a chapter which highlights different individuals 'finding" Christ, Anna's life circumstances had afforded her a unique perspective and appreciation in finding Him. Likewise, the Lord has framed all the circumstances of our lives to provide a window through which we can learn His heart in fresh ways.

She "served God with fasting and prayer, night and day" (2:37). The word which the Spirit of God employs for her "service" suggests spiritual or religious service. He elevates what she did to an almost priestly activity. As well the Spirit's commendation shows her commitment and consistency – fasting and prayer, and night and day. God has nothing positive to say about the architectural accomplishment of the temple that reflected Herod's skill. It is silent about the priests and Levites, scribes, and Pharisees. But it does devote these three verses and 85 words as a tribute to this widow.

Her Witness

We read concerning Anna that "she spake of Him to all them that looked for redemption in Jerusalem." Though she departed not from the temple, she was in touch with a godly remnant. She knew who was in touch with heaven and who was looking for the Redeemer to come. Here was a widow who gathered around herself a group of like-minded believers in the nation, those who were expecting a Redeemer. The value of friendship is stressed throughout the book of Proverbs. The importance of choosing friends who can serve as spiritual help is vital. This small coterie of friends found their joy in the news of the Redeemer.

She stands in contrast to Simeon who came in and praised and worshiped the child, giving thanks to God. Then he turned to Mary and Joseph and blessed them. Anna, however, went out to others and told them of the Babe Who had come. Both of these exercises are earmarks of believers: telling the Father of His Son and telling others of the Redeemer. Recall that Jacob, in his patriarchal-prophetic blessing on his sons, spoke of Asher that his "bread shall be fat" and as yielding "royal dainties" (Gen 49:20). Anna, true to her tribal prophecy, was providing food for spiritual sustenance.

A consideration of a widow and the spiritual profit of her words should cause all of us to ponder our words. Do I provide bread and "dainties" for the people of God, not just when preaching, but as part of conversation? God intends us to edify (1 Thess 5:11), exhort (Heb 3:13), encourage (1 Thess 4:18), and to provoke one another to good works (Heb 10:24). There are almost 15 different "one another" imperatives in the New Testament.

All of these ministries are not only "platform" exercises. The vast majority of this type of service "one to another" is done in conversation, by letter, or other means of private interaction. We have the potential to encourage or to discourage by our words. A ministry of encouragement is of inestimable value among the people of God.

Her Worth

I fully appreciate a gap of 12 years between verse 38 and verse 41. Yet, keeping mind that Luke has arranged his events in a moral and not chronological order, there may well be a lesson to be learned. In verses 41-45, we have the story of the family's visit to Jerusalem to attend the Passover, a requirement of all the Jewish males. Just prior to this, in the moral order of Luke's writing, the Lord Jesus is spoken of as the Redeemer. We then have the seeming anomaly that the Redeemer Himself is going up to Jerusalem to celebrate the historical redemption of the nation. Could the Spirit of God in this manner, be reminding us that the boy of 12 going up to the Passover, was the ultimate Redemption prefigured in the Exodus from Egypt? He Himself needed no "Passover" as all would be fulfilled in Him. Later in his gospel, Luke will tell us of the events which transpired on the Mount of Transfiguration. There, with Moses and Elijah, the theme of the conversation was the "Exodus" that He would accomplish in Jerusalem (Luke 9:31).

Anna, prepared by the seemingly adverse circumstances of life, was introducing the antitype of the Passover to the nation. Mary had brought the antitype in her arms as she brought her offering (2:22-24). The burnt and sin offerings were being replaced by the Saviour; Anna was telling of One Who would fulfil the great Passover deliverance spiritually for His people.

Did Anna realise all she was doing? I do not know. But he Spirit of God elevates her service, even though summarised in three verses, and inscribes an eternal memorial to the widow of the temple.

Barzillai

"Friendship isn't about who you've known the longest, it's about who walked into your life, said 'I'm here for you' and proved it."

Anonymous

Reading: *2 Samuel 19:31-39*

His Worth

Barzillai graces the pages of Scripture in a very dark day in David's life. David had known other similar days, but this has to rank near the top for its tragic and heart-breaking events. A usurper had seized the throne. Intensifying his sorrow, it was actually his son, Absalom. The result was that David was fleeing for his life. It is against the landscape of this rebellion that Barzillai is introduced.

We are told a number of details about this patriot. His origin was across the Jordan. He was an aged man, one of Scriptures' octogenarians, 80 years of age, and we are told that he was a very great man (2 Sam 19:32). Only a few men in Scripture have this attached to their names: Isaac became very great (Gen 26:13). The man Moses was very great (Ex 11:3); even Nabal is referred to in this way, likely for his riches and prosperity (1 Sam 25:2). Finally, Job had the distinction of being the greater of all the men of the east (Job 1:3).

"Greatness" in most of these passages refers to material wealth. In the case of Barzillai, it also reveals to us his moral wealth. In a dark day, here was a man who stood up for David when family and friends forsook him. He had little connection with the tribe of Judah. His home was east of Jordan. He could easily have remained neutral in the conflict or have waited to see how the battle would go. But instead, he came to meet David along with two other men (one a man who was an Ammonite) and brought David and his army much needed supplies.

Standing for the Lord Jesus, standing for the truth of God, and representing Him in a dark day must bring Him joy. We bemoan the character of our day. The apathy, the moral darkness, and stark Biblical illiteracy, plus the secular society in which we are found combine to make gospel work very difficult. But God has placed us here, now, in this day, to represent Him and His interests. We are not privileged to choose the time or the place in which we can live and maintain testimony for God. That is all in God's providence. "The lot is cast into the lap; but the whole disposing thereof is of the LORD" (Pro 16:33). But we can be faithful and, like a Barzillai, stand with David in his rejection.

It is also significant that this man did his greatest work at 80 years of age. He was not living in the past. He was still seeking to do what he could for the Lord and for His anointed. Many of us view the senior years as a time to relax, sit back, and reminisce. Of course, added to it is a good dose of criticism of the current generation who are not up to the standard we set! But Barzillai moved in fellowship with two others to meet a crisis. He could not sit idly by as the true king was in rejection.

He also stood with David when the fate of the battle was unknown. Had Absalom triumphed, Barzillai was certain to face death. Yet he was willing to be committed to David whatever the cost. Like Ittai, he might well have said, "whether in life or death even there also will thy servant be" (2 Sam 15:21).

Unlike Barzillai, we know how the battle will end. We have read the end of the story and know that one day the King will return to reign. How much more should we be willing to be linked with Him in His rejection.

His Wealth

His Good Sense

David, his family, and his army had to flee in haste. Likely, they did not have provisions and the much needed supplies for the time away from Jerusalem. Barzillai sensed the need and met it in abundance. It may well be that the followers of David numbered in the thousands. The need was great. Yet Barzillai met it abundantly.

It is wonderful to have believers in an assembly who can sense need. The need may be for a word in season from the Scriptures or for a loaf of bread from the oven. The needs of the believers are many and varied. The things brought to David in the day of his rejection were far more valuable than jewels and gold. They met a present need. They recognised that "the people are hungry, and weary, and thirsty" (2 Sam 17:29).

To be a believer with sensitivity to need and the wisdom to meet that need requires spiritual exercise in the presence of God. The assembly at Philippi sensed the need of the apostle imprisoned in Rome. The apostle sensed in turn the need of the poor saints in Jerusalem for material things and stirred the believers in Achaia to meet that need. The wise woman of Shunem could discern the need of the prophet. And then there is the constant need that many believers have for a word of encouragement. A "gift" such as this can only be developed from fellowship with the Lord.

His Great Expense

In 2 Samuel 17:27-29 we read, "And it came to pass, when David was come to Mahanaim, that Shobi the son of Nahash of Rabbah of the children of Ammon, and Machir the son of Ammiel of Lodebar, and Barzillai the Gileadite of Rogelim, brought beds, and basons, and earthen vessels, and wheat, and barley, and flour, and parched corn, and beans, and lentils, and parched pulse, And honey, and butter, and sheep, and cheese of kine, for David, and for the people that were with him, to eat: for they said, The people is hungry, and weary, and thirsty, in the wilderness."

Notice how the spirit of God details and itemises everything. The repetition of the word "and" makes each gift a special offering. Nothing is lumped together but each item is mentioned, tabulated, and recognised for its worth. It is similar to the Lord's recompense of His servants in Mark 10:30.

I doubt if lentils would have been a prized gift when David was on the throne; beds and basons would have been of little value when David was in the palace. Beans and barley, the food of the poor, might have even been viewed as an insult to present to a king. Now, however, they took on a value far greater than their intrinsic monetary worth. The darkness and danger of the day made the sacrifice very significant to David.

Barzillai was "a very great man," suggesting to us his material abundance. But he employed that wealth for David. Nothing appears to have been held back; all was supplied for David and his men. There are believers to whom God has entrusted material possessions. It is part of their stewardship to employ that wealth for the kingdom of God. Barzillai contrasts with another very great man, Nabal, who refused to give of his abundance to meet the need of David's men in the wilderness. It turned out to be very costly for him to act in such a miserly and selfish fashion. He lost all in the end. Similarly, if we fail in our stewardship, we will lose eternally.

Gospel work, both at home and on the mission field, has become increasingly expensive. Renting property for meetings now comes with the additional expense of liability insurance which many are required to obtain to protect the owner. The cost to advertise the meetings is also significant. In short, the work of God and the gospel requires believers who will support that work with the abundance that the Lord has given to them.

His Singular Recompense

A day came when the king returned. Barzillai was obviously looking forward to that day. As soon as he heard that the king was going to cross back over the Jordan, Barzillai met him. David had great things to offer him for his faithfulness. But Barzillai refused all that the king had to offer, but he did receive a reward that he must have cherished until his dying day. We read simply, "the king kissed Barzillai and blessed him" (2 Sam 19:39). A kiss from the king was all that Barzillai sought when the day of reward came.

Am I looking for the "return of the King?" Would a kiss from the King compensate me for anything sacrificed or done for Him? Will I be a Nabal or a Barzillai?

His Wish

I must rush here to the defense of Barzillai. Many commentators are critical of his words in 2 Samuel 19 when David offers him a place back in Jerusalem. They view Barzillai's words as excuses – his age, decreased ability to enjoy the blessings of the king's provision, his protestation of being a burden to the king. The words of Barzillai actually breathe an air of contentment. He is not looking for greatness or a special place at David's table. He is content to dwell among his own people and finish his days where the Lord had placed him. His words remind us of the great woman of Shunem when confronted with a similar request: "Behold, thou hast been careful for us with all this care; what is to be done for thee? wouldest thou be spoken for to the king, or to the captain of the host? And she answered, I dwell among mine own people" (2 Kings 4:13).

There is a beauty to a believer nearing the end of life marked by a spirit of contentment. There are always regrets and things we would love to do over, but to come to life's end and feel that, like Paul, "I have finished my course," and as it was said of John the Baptiser, "And as John fulfilled his course," is a blessing indeed.

Barzillai did have one request. It concerned his desire for his son, Chimham. He wanted him to enjoy the bounty of the king's table. That is a worthy desire for every Christian parent. His wish was granted as Chimham was seated at David's table and this blessing continued into the reign of Solomon as David charged his son (1 Kings 2:7). David remembered with deep appreciation that, "they (Barzillai) came to me when I fled because of Absalom thy brother." The kindness of Barzillai was not easily forgotten even by the aged king.

There is one additional intriguing mention of Chimham found in Jeremiah's writings. When Johanan and the small remnant that was left after the Chaldean invasion and the evil of Ishmael, made their way to Egypt, they stopped at the habitation (literally, the inn) of Chimham that was by Bethlehem (Jer 41:17). An inn at Bethlehem is certainly something that triggers many questions in our minds.

Barzillai joins a long list of those believers who appear for a very brief time, cameo appearances in the long history of the world, but they accomplished far more than they were able to appreciate. How thankful we should be that their record is inscribed on the inspired page for all eternity!

Benaiah

"Do all the good you can, by all the means you can, in all the ways you can, in all the places you can, at all the times you can, to all the people you can, as long as ever you can."

John Wesley

Reading: *2 Samuel 23:13-23*

God's Preparation

His Influence

Benaiah is introduced to us in 2 Samuel 8, but it is not until we come to the close of David's life and the recounting of his mighty men, that we learn a vital truth. There we read, of "Benaiah, the son of Jehoiada, a valiant man" (2 Sam 23:20). I would understand from this, that his father, Jehoiada was a valiant man. We are reminded of the influence a parent can have on a child. We cannot presume upon God, and it must be added that many mighty men and women of God have not had the joy of seeing their children follow in their steps, but it is the responsibility of each to so live that the children following do have an example to follow. Jehoiada provided just such an example for his son. Benaiah rose to equal feats of valor and might in the service of God.

Individuals Who Have Matriculated

Benaiah was enrolled in the school of God, whether he knew it or not. Despite the credentials of a valiant father and his lineage, he had to learn responsibility and learn God for himself. His first mention indicates that he was given a position of responsibility over the Cherethites and the Pelethites (2 Sam 8:18). While a place of importance, it did not place him at the top of David's list of mighty men. He had charge of a group of men who appear to have been non-Israelites, but who were devoted to David and his safety. Possibly they comprised a private "body-guard" for David.

If this is the case, then Benaiah learned devotion to the person of David before he became involved in battles for the king. He would serve in a capacity of importance, but less so than the glory of the three mighty men who must have captured the imagination and admiration of all the youth of Israel.

God always prepares His servants for the task He intends ultimately to assign to them.

Elijah must know the place of dependence, being fed by ravens and then by a Gentile widow. Abram must experience famine and testing. Noah would have to wait patiently in the ark with no word from God as to when the deluge would end and his ultimate fate.

Importance of the Lessons

Benaiah learned responsibility in one sphere before he was advanced to another. Before he was given charge for all of David and then Solomon's army, he was in charge of only the personal guard. Also, as far as his trials were concerned, this principle was also in operation. He faced two lion-like men before he faced the lion (2 Sam 23:20). He was taught devotion to David and was close enough to David to hear the whispers of his heart for a drink of water from the well at Bethlehem (2 Sam 23:13-17). Only devotion to the person of David would inspire such an act. That same devotion would enable him to do something greater than breaking through hosts of Philistines. A day would come when he would have to move quickly and wisely to secure the throne for Solomon, opposing Joab and Adonijah.

God always prepares His servants. Abram began his education with the lesson that God could bring life out of a dead womb and his own dead body (Rom 4:19-21). His God was the kind of God Who could bring life out of death. That truth was what enabled him to walk up the mountain in Moriah with the assurance that, "I and the lad will go yonder and worship and come again to you" (Gen 22:5). The God he served could raise Isaac from the ashes!

The Lord taught His disciples in the same manner. He first took them to the sea of Galilee and was with them, asleep in the boat. When the storm arose, He arose and rebuked it, assuring them of their safety when they obeyed His command (Matt 8:23-27). But on the next occasion, He was not with them in the boat. They were on their own. But they had His Word to go (Matt 14:22). Again, a storm arose, testing their faith. Was the Lord as faithful when on the mount as when with them in the boat? The test of their faith was to their shame; but they were learning Him on each occasion.

In a similar manner, the Lord teaches us, making each test of our confidence in Him a little more difficult. He deals very gently with new believers, often answering prayer very quickly. Older, mature saints are made to wait, depending on God amidst the darkness at times.

God's Personal Attention

God educates each of us in a different and unique manner. Your lessons are not mine. He is a skilled and wise mentor. He fashions our lessons to meet our needs and His goal for our lives.

Variety of Lessons:

Benaiah faced a variety of foes. There were the two lion-like men of Moab. Then there was a lion in a pit in a time of snow. That was followed by an Egyptian with superior armament. Finally, he had to face Adonijah and Joab and a rebellion against God's choice of Solomon. Here were formidable foes indeed! These were not the same trials which Shammah and Eleazar had to face. Even Abishai who seems to be comrade with Benaiah as one of the "second" three did not have these experiences.

The Venue

The circumstances of our trials are also unique. Two believers may have the same type of trial, but the circumstances and backgrounds can vary so that each is unique to them. It is noteworthy that God makes mention of the place, time, and conditions which Benaiah faced when confronted with the lion. Curiosity wants to ask how he got into the pit, but the lesson for us is found elsewhere. It was a pit; it was a time of snow. God saw the circumstances in which Benaiah did his heroic deed. But beyond the deed, the circumstances elevated its value. It has been said and said well, "The day defines the deed." And then, he not only slew an Egyptian but did so with the Egyptian's own spear, a deed of no mean significance.

The Value of the lessons

A reading of 2 Samuel 23:13-17 does not guarantee that Benaiah was part of the three who broke through Philistine ranks to honour David, but it is strongly suggestive. So, allow me an author's pardon if I ascribe this act to to him, as well as Abishai and possibly Asahel. Here were men close enough to David to know what would please him. Here were men who risked their lives, not to fulfill the command of David, but the desire of David. It seems significant that Joab, always calculating what was best for himself, was not among these three.

We are given precepts that we are called upon to obey. Imperatives fill the epistles, giving us light for our journey here. But then there are things that are not commanded but are ways in which we can please Him. May we each rise to that level of spiritual living.

Virtue Displayed

Benaiah stands in contrast to Joab, the general whom he would one day replace. With Benaiah, there is no sign of rivalry or self-interest. His motivation is devotion to David. While we must admit that it is unlikely we ever rise to the heights of absolutely pure motivation, we can strive to be pure in our hearts to the degree that we can be. Corinth was marred by a competitive spirit. Something of the same but perhaps for other reasons marked the readers to whom James wrote (James 4). We long to be significant and can even use a spiritual veneer to cover our ambition and competitiveness. Benaiah stands as an example of a man who was content with his role until God chose to advance him.

God's Passing Grades

Benaiah faced a number of challenges and foes as we have mentioned. Commentators and preachers often point out the nature of the three foes:

There was the test of Moab a consistent picture throughout Scripture of the flesh. The Egyptian reminds us of the world we face, giant-like in its opposition. The lion, of course, is a depiction of Satan in his fury (1 Pet 5:8). Benaiah confronted and defeated all of these. His usefulness for David was seen in his victories over all that would oppose the believer.

One of the realities is that in the school of God, graduation day does not come until the end of the journey. Benaiah would still have to face Adonijah and the rebellion. Joab, once his superior, would be part of that conspiracy. Benaiah would ultimately have the solemn and sad responsibility of executing Joab, Adonijah, and Shimei. He proved faithful to David and then to Solomon. His concern was for the rightful man to be upon the throne and have the devotion of the people of God.

Godly men seek to direct the affections and attention of believers to the Lord in the midst. His honour and glory are what are preeminent in the hearts of such.

God's Promotion

Loyalty Applauded

David recognised his value and valour. He rewarded him by promotion and honour. When he came to make up his honour role of mighty men, Benaiah had his place, not only named, but described with his deeds detailed. 2 Samuel 23, along with Genesis 49, Romans 16, and Nehemiah 3, all serve as previews of the Judgment Seat of Christ. What a reminder there is here in David's list of mighty men, that no act of devotion done for the Lord will be forgotten at the Bema.

Labour Appreciated

As a result of his faithfulness in his exploits, Benaiah was placed above the 30 even though not among the first three. He was also given charge of the guard. He had proved faithful and was gradually brought into spheres of greater responsibility and usefulness.

Likeness Attained

He is the most like David of any of the 37 mighty men. Consider this: he slew a lion and David slew a lion and bear. He slew a giant with a spear and David slew Goliath with his sword. But there were limits as well: this giant was 5 cubits; Goliath was 6 cubits. This giant had a spear, Goliath had a sword of which there was none like it. Trials are allowed to bring us into greater spheres of usefulness and likeness to Christ. The trials through which Benaiah passed made him increasingly like David. In each trial we learn God in a fresh manner, and are brought into greater likeness to the Son.

Benaiah was certainly a man who followed John Wesley's dictum and did all the good he could all the days of his life. How refreshing to see a man who began well, went on well, and finished even better.

Dorcas

"Live so as to be Missed"

Reading: *Acts 9:36-42*

Her Life

Dorcas, "doe or gazelle," takes centre stage at the end of Acts 9. We are not privy to the circumstances of her life. Was she a widow herself? Was she aged or young? The seeming burden of the believers for her at her death suggests that she may have had an untimely death. If so, it reminds us that the Lord takes some of the most useful servants home much earlier than we expect.

One thing is certain, that her death represented a loss to the believers whom she served.

The Lord also had another purpose in the events surrounding Dorcas. In His sovereignty He brought Peter to a place only a short distance away, perhaps 10 miles to the NW. God had something more to display through the life of this sister. God was also bringing Peter to Joppa to make him available, not only for Dorcas but for the momentous events of the next chapter, the gospel going out to Gentiles (Acts 10).

His grace had been displayed in her life; now the greatness of His power was to be displayed in her return to life. He does not always work in this way. It may seem strange to some that amidst the history changing events detailed in the book of Acts, the "turning of the world upside down," that this rather local matter is related.

Some will suggest, and rightly so, that the structure of the book of Acts shows the parallel ministry of Peter in chapters 1-12 with that of Paul which occupies the remainder of the book. Paul will raise one to life in chapter 20 and Peter's activity is seen here, paralleling that in his raising of Dorcas. But perhaps, along with the parallelism of the book, there is another and more practical lesson to be gleaned.

There may be in the story of Dorcas, preparation for Peter for the events in the home of Cornelius. It is interesting that in the healing of Aeneas, we are told that Peter came down to the saints. In the raising of Dorcas, he presented her to the saints. These two mentions of saints are among only four in the entire account of the Acts. Also, in the healing and raising of Aeneas, Peter helped a man who could do no good works. In the case of Dorcas, she was full of good works. Yet both needed the power of God. Cornelius will be introduced to us as man who gave "much alms" and who "worked righteousness" (v 35); he also needed the power of God in conversion.

Her Location

It was Jonah, about eight centuries earlier, who put Joppa on the map. For him, it was the starting point of a journey away from God. His adventure led to the salvation of the sailors and then the men of Nineveh. He was full of self-pity and anger, Dorcas was full of good works. In the story of Jonah there is a symbolic or metaphorical death and resurrection (Matt 12:40). In Dorcas, there is a literal death and recalling to life.

Her Labour

She was a follower - A disciple.

She is the only woman in Scripture so described as a disciple. Does this give us some insight into her personal piety and devotion? If so, it is significant that her character is noted before her service. It is reminiscent of Ezra who was called "the priest, the scribe." He was a man of the sanctuary and then a man of the Scriptures; he was in the presence of God before being in the public eye.

God is far more interested in the work He is doing in us, conforming us to His Son, than in the work that we are doing for Him. Character is what is important to God. The Lord told those He called, "Follow Me, and I will make you ..."

There are believers who, due to circumstances beyond their control, cannot serve as they would desire. They have limitations of health, age, or of personal things in life. Yet each of us is able to allow the Spirit of God to work in us and change us into greater conformity to God's Son, even if He is not able to work through us as we might desire.

She is described as fruitful - Full of good works and alms deeds.

Her good deeds appear to be the coats and garments which she had made for the widows of the assembly. Paul wrote to the Ephesians assembly that God saved us with a view to good works, which God "foreordained that we should walk in them" (Eph 2:10). Among the many reasons grace has touched your life and mine is that we might reflect the character of a God who is "good" by doing "good" works. While we are told to think of the needs of believers first of all (Gal 6:10), our "good" God makes His rain to fall on the just and unjust in equal quantities (Matt 7:27). We should maintain good works (Titus 3:1) in society, without becoming involved in social movements and protests.

Any mention of good works draws our minds to the epistle of Titus and the six mentions of good works which dot the landscape of that letter. The people to whom Paul was writing were, in their unconverted days, characterised as being lazy, liars, and lawless. The grace of God that had appeared bringing salvation was intended to empower, motivate, and change them.

In Paul's first two mentions of good works, we learn that they are an imperative for leaders. They were lacking in the professors (1:16) but required in the leaders (2:7). In the next couplet, they are the intention of Calvary's work (2:14; 3:1). In the final couplet, good works are seen as important to practical Christianity (3:8, 14).

Dorcas practiced copious Christianity as she was "full" of good works and alms deeds. She did not serve out of duty or duress; she was serving out of devotion to her Lord.

She is described as faithful - Which she did.

She did not merely think about something she could do to honour the Lord. She did it. The burden and opportunity which the Lord gave her may not have seemed spectacular or important. She was content to serve in a small and seemingly insignificant manner. It is vital to see needs which exist in the assembly and in gospel work. It is even more important to address those needs and to be active in the needed labour. Dorcas was not a consultant to the work of the Lord, she was a labourer.

Her Legacy

She left the fruits of her labours which were obvious for all to see. None of us will have a recall to life if the Lord calls us home. Yet the question still begs to be answered, "What is the legacy that I will leave?" There was visible fruit that followed her death.

Not all fruit will be seen this side of eternity. We are reminded that in gospel work, we sow, and others may reap. In ministry and teaching, we are investing in the future of believers and the assembly. Fruit may not be obvious to us. All that understood, it is still true that we are going to pass on a legacy to our families and fellow believers. Acts of kindness, sacrifices made for others, an exemplary life – these are some of the aspects of the legacy we are going to leave behind.

People will not mention the big home or the expensive car, the exotic holidays or designer clothes, they will call to mind the character of the person who has been taken from them.

The Loss

With the death of Dorcas, the believers in Joppa, knowing of Peter's presence only ten miles away, sent for him. Was this to comfort the saints? To be present at her burial? Or did they think that, like his Master, he might be able to recall her to life? We are not told.

Peter arrived and put everyone out of the room, wishing to be alone with God and the woman, reminiscent of Elisha (2 Kings 4). He lifted his voice to God in prayer, owning his dependence upon a power outside of himself. Turning to the damsel, he said, "Tabitha arise." It is almost what the Lord said in Mark 5:41, "Talitha cumi." Divine power called her back to continue her service in Joppa, and to be the means, not only of good works, but of the good report that led to many being saved (v 42).

The Lessons

These seven verses of Scripture are replete with lessons for us:

- The sovereign ways of God with His servants, both Dorcas and Peter
- The legacy that we will leave behind
- Contentment to labour in the background and serve the needs of those who cannot repay in kind
- The importance of good works

Ebed-melech and Baruch

"Wherever you are, be all there"

Jim Elliot

Reading: *Jeremiah 38:7-13; 39:15-18; 36:1-10; 45*

Allow me to justify why these two men deserve a page or two in the chronicle of minor lives. That they are minor, no one would debate. Baruch occupies no more than dozen or so verses; Ebed-melech even fewer. But are they "significant" enough in their insignificance to be included? They deserve to be together since they were both associated with Jeremiah in his lonely ministry for the Lord. Also, they possibly represent the only two converts, the fruit from many years of faithful ministry by that prophet. Each served in a different manner, and yet each of them was useful to the prophet in his labour and life.

They also served as companions and perhaps encouragements to a man to whom God forbad the comfort and consolations of marriage. Jeremiah had no wife to whom he could return at the close of a difficult day of testimony for God. But he did have a Baruch in whom he might have found comfort and companionship. In Ebed-melech, there was someone who was marked by the fear of God, and had sympathy for the prophet, a quality sadly lacking in the remainder of the nation.

Ebed-melech

The Man

Ebed-melech is the O. T. Ethiopian Eunuch. As in the case of the more famous N. T. Ethiopian eunuch, he rose above the nation of his origin. He rose above the standard of the society in which he resided. And he also rose above the atmosphere of the court of King Zedekiah.

He appeared suddenly upon the page in Scripture in Jeremiah 38. The circumstances are well known. The weak and vacillating king had imprisoned Jeremiah at the insistence of his court. Jeremiah sank in the mire and was left literally to die. Ebed-melech courageously confronted the king and asked for Jeremiah's life. Possibly Ebed-melech was a court attendant, a servant of the king in some capacity. But for a lowly court slave to challenge the actions of the more powerful princes, knowing full-well how unreliable Zedekiah was, revealed a moral strength that was a welcome visitor into the court of this wicked and pusillanimous king.

He serves as a fitting reminder of the need to be willing to rise above what is of nature and what is natural. It is contrary to our flesh to be different, to stand out and stand up for what is right. But in every generation, those who have been used of God have had to dare to be different, to refuse to bend and blend with the society around them.

His Ministry

Against the background of the horrific danger and calamity which faced the city and the nation, the action of this man would seem very small. Delivering one man from a dungeon pit and remitting him to the court of the prison certainly did not send shock waves through the spiritual fibre of the nation. Strangely, there seemed to be little reaction to it as described in the text. Just one man whose conditions were bettered; one man who was saved from starvation and death. It was a small deed against the landscape of the history of the prophets. Yet it was a deed noted by the Lord and recorded to Ebed-melech's honour for eternity.

We "rate" the value of service by its size and success. We need to be conscious that God's rating system is far different. He values faithfulness, and the darker the day, the greater the deed. It must have thrilled the heart of God that amidst the decadence of the nation, when no Israelite stepped forward to help the prophet, that there was a foreigner who had trusted God through Jeremiah's ministry and who did act decisively for God.

Just as the oft-repeated words of the Lord Jesus concerning a cup of cold water given in His Name and its attendant reward are true, so every act, done in devotion to Him, is noted and compensated by the Just Judge.

The Manner

Scripture is frequently careful to record not only what was done for the Lord, but how it was done. The small details are important with God. We read that Ebed-melech took 30 men and "old cast clouts and rotten rags" to draw Jeremiah up out of the pit. Not only would he help him, but he would seek to do it in the least painful way possible and in the safest way he could. He instructed Jeremiah to put the old rags under his under armpits under the cords, to cushion the effect on his body.

We learn once again that God not only takes note of the action, but of the motive and manner. Ebed-melech sought not only to do a good thing, but to do it in the best possible way. The Perfect Servant not only knew what to say to those in need, but "how" to speak a word in season (Isa 50:4). He not only healed the leper but touched Him to convey that healing.

Ebed-melech "lifted" a man from a pit. There are believers whom God has gifted to be able to "lift" other believers, either by private or public ministry. The have the right words, they say them in the right manner, and they are said at the perfect season. Be a believer who can lift another out of a pit of despair or discouragement.

The Motive

It seems when reading Jeremiah 38, that Ebed-melech's faithfulness goes unnoticed by heaven. But we need to turn the page. The next chapter tells us of a message delivered to Jeremiah while in the court of the prison. He, in turn, was to speak the message to Ebed-melech. God had taken notice of his action. God did see into his heart and knew the motive for his courageous deed.

It is interesting that the God who sent the message to Ebed-melech the Ethiopian is called here the God Israel. It is as though God recognised that here was a foreigner who was acting with more spiritual grace than any in the nation. And God recognised and appreciated that he had "put thy trust in Me, saith the Lord" (v 18).

The result of this faithfulness and trust was that, unlike the nation, his life would be spared when the enemy prevailed, and the city capitulated. God appreciated the deed of kindness done to His servant.

Though none of us can ever boast of a totally pure motive, we should seek to move with as pure a motive, as consecrated a desire, as is possible. This is what brings pleasure to the heart of God.

While we come short, it is thrilling to muse upon the One Man Whose every motive was totally selfless and God-honouring. Oh, for a heart transplant if it were possible!

Baruch

Baruch is introduced to us in Jeremiah 32 as Jeremiah's secretary or scribe. Why Jeremiah needed a scribe is not revealed. He seemed to fulfil a prosaic role in the drama of Jeremiah's life, yet he should not be dismissed as insignificant. Jewish historians such as Josephus tell us that he came from a very distinguished and influential family. This sounds feasible especially in light of his access to the court and his initial acceptance by the princes. From the responsibilities delegated to him, certain things can be inferred.

The Confidence Jeremiah Had in Him

In chapter 36:4, Baruch wrote the words which came from the lips of Jeremiah. Then, he is instructed by Jeremiah to read the words to the people on "fasting day." Two challenges to faithfulness are seen here: he had to record the words faithfully, and then he had to speak them in truth to all the people. What followed is the famous incident of Jehoiakim and his penknife. The king and his court had little interest in the Word of God. Unlike previous kings in Judah, he did not rend his clothes and cry out to God; he "rent" the Scriptures. It was in this atmosphere that Baruch was faithful. The courage to stand forth and speak the Word of God, a message that would be unpopular, tells us something of the character of Baruch.

Jeremiah knew the mettle of the man and had confidence that, though shut up in the prison, the message would be conveyed accurately to the nation.

In an earlier chapter but a later period of time, Baruch was charged with another responsibility. Jeremiah was imprisoned and the remarkable story of the purchase of the field from Uncle Hanameel is played out. The evidence of the purchased field is given to Baruch. He is delegated to place it into an earthen vessel to authenticate and preserve the proof of the purchase in light of the future. Once again, he carried out the request of Jeremiah, displaying his confidence in the future for the nation.

Can God turn to me with confidence? Will I be faithful with the message of God to my generation? In the gospel? In teaching all the Word of God? Can others in the assembly look to me with confidence or am I an unreliable person?

The Circumstances He Knew

As a result of faithfulness with God's Word and his fidelity to Jeremiah, on one occasion he was forced into hiding along with Jeremiah (36:26). Then, he was falsely accused by the princes who claimed that Baruch had made Jeremiah prophesy against their traveling to Egypt. Finally, he shared the fate of the man he represented, as he accompanied Jeremiah into exile in Egypt (43:2, 3).

Faithfulness came with a cost. Baruch endured hardness for the sake of another (2 Tim 2:3). Representing Jeremiah, the reproaches that the people had for his master fell on him. The same is true in our day if we are to be found faithful.

The Counsel of God to Him

Chapter 45 of Jeremiah is a chapter devoted to God's message to Baruch. It was actually delivered earlier in the life of Baruch, coinciding with the fourth year of Jehoiakim. It is inserted here as an introduction to what follows in chapter 46-51 as God pronounces judgment upon the surrounding nations.

In this brief chapter we see Baruch's sorrow, in fact sorrow upon sorrow. Was his sorrow in fellowship with Jeremiah who wept over the sinful condition of the nation and its impending judgment? Was it the sorrow that all his expectations for usefulness and blessing to the nation (seeking great things) were never to materialise? Possibly, like his brother Seraiah (51:59), he aspired to a place of usefulness in the court of the king. But Seraiah would know captivity in Babylon in association with King Zedekiah. Baruch's life was spared. Whatever the case, the Lord was sensitive to his grief and to the burden of his heart. There seems, however, to be in the words of God to Baruch, a sense that God also has had his hope for the nation changed. Of course, with God there are no disappointment or surprises, but there is genuine sorrow. But He speaks in sympathy to Baruch that what He had built and what He Himself had planted is going to be pulled down and plucked up. He will also know something of grief over the future.

Yet, amidst this, God makes a similar promise to Baruch as He did to Ebed-Melech: "Thy life will I give unto the for a prey in all places whither thou goest" (45:5). God would honour the faithfulness of His servant.

All of this sends our minds back to Peter's admonitions. We live in a world under the judgment of God, a world that is moving toward its own destruction. In light of this, our lives should be marked by holiness and "not seeking great things for ourselves."

Elisabeth

"Faith goes up the stairs that love has built and looks out the
windows which hope has opened."

Charles H. Spurgeon

Reading: *Luke 1:5-45*

Luke begins his gospel by introducing us to several couples marked
by godliness of character. They form part of a remnant who reflect the
character of Malachi 3: "Then they that feared the Lord spake often
one to another, and the Lord hearkened and heard it" (Mal 3:16). The
last word of the prophet had faded from the ears of men 400 years
earlier. But here is a group who are still living in the atmosphere of
Malachi's Words. Here was a small nucleus of Jewish believers seeking
to live and honour God amidst the barren and bankrupt conditions of
the nation as a whole. Zacharias the priest and his wife, Elisabeth, are
among this small group. To them Luke will add Joseph and Mary, and
Simeon and Anna. Only six, but think of what these six accomplished
for God!

Yet, as is almost universally true, it was not accomplished without
sacrifice and suffering in some form. As the curtain opens on the
gospel of Luke, we find Zacharias in the temple, serving according
to his lot, and Elisabeth likely at home in the hill country (possibly
Hebron). The same God Who began the nation with an old couple,
past child-bearing years, Abram and Sarai, is about to work again in
the nation with another aged couple likewise past child-bearing years.
God seems to specialise in unusual births!

The Adversity She Encountered

Her Moral Character

We are introduced to Elisabeth and Zacharias and told of their piety and practice. They are described as righteous before the Lord and blameless before others. They are walking in all the commandments of the Lord, careful with every Word of God. Theirs was not a mere outward superficial veneer to impress others. There was reality found in both husband and wife.

Elisabeth is depicted as a woman who feared the Lord, supporting her husband, and faithfully serving as she is able. She was righteous before God, her piety, and blamelessness before men, her practice.

Luke, who is going to present the Lord Jesus as a Perfect Man, begins his record with a reminder that God is looking for reality in His people. Hypocrites, especially of the religious variety, will be encountered throughout this gospel, but we begin with a woman who was genuine in every sense. In linking together her inward piety with her outward practice, her life Godward and her life manward, we are being reminded that the inner life should control the outer life. What I am in the presence of God should determine what I am before men. In a day when the cry of many is that the outward is of no consequence, we need to remember that the outward reflects and reveals the inner.

Her Marriage

Their marriage was "in the Lord." Zacharias had not only married within the tribe of Levi, but had taken a daughter of Aaron. They are seen moving together in their prayerful exercise before God. They had continued in marriage for many years as is obvious from their longing for a child and their advanced age.

God's intention is for marriage to be a permanent life-long commitment. That commitment will be tested by all the selfishness that resides within our flesh, the evils and standards of a society around us, and the stratagems of the evil one (1 Cor 7:5). Every married couple must be aware of all that is arrayed against their marriage, and cry to the Lord for preservation.

The Mark Against Her

Despite the piety which marked this saint of old, she knew heartache and grief. She was barren. Not only were the natural longings of a woman's heart never satisfied, but in the culture of the day it carried the added opprobrium that it indicated the judgment of God for hidden sin. She knew reproach all her life to this point in time. A righteous life did not preclude sorrows and tears. No doubt long months and year passed as hope began to fade for a child. Each year passed with the increasing reproach of what barrenness meant. With the announcement of the angel to Zacharias, she owned that God had taken "away my reproach from among men" (Luke 1:25). Two women, Mary and Elisabeth, learned of the birth of their sons within the same chapter. But for Elisabeth, it meant the removal of reproach; for Mary, it meant the acceptance of reproach.

"Thy prayer is heard" (Luke 1:13). What did this mean? Had their prayers for a child from years earlier been stored up in God's "pending file?" Was it a prayer for the nation and its recovery? Whatever the case, we are reminded that prayers are answered in God's time and on His terms. It would require a Caesar on the throne to issue his edict, a young teenager in Nazareth old enough to conceive a Son, and "the fullness of the times" having arrived. God's timing is always perfect even when He seems to be late!

The Ministry of Encouragement

Her Confession and Its Implications

Picture once again the scene: Mary having just conceived in the womb, hastens to visit her relative, Elisabeth. At this point in time, there would be no external evidence of her having conceived. Yet, before a word is uttered or any announcement is made, Elisabeth blesses her and speaks of the fruit of her womb. Was Mary startled at this?

But it goes even further when Elisabeth speaks of the Babe in the womb as "My Lord." What a confession to make! Elisabeth recognises the uniqueness of the Babe in the womb as she owns Him as her Lord. Five individuals in Scripture own the Lord Jesus by this title, "My Lord." David before His birth (Ps 110:1), Elisabeth at His birth, Mary thinking He was dead (John 20:13), Thomas in resurrection (John 20:28), and the Apostle Paul in ascended glory (Phil 3:8).

Elisabeth's character is displayed here in glowing colours. For Elisabeth, the pregnancy and birth of her son who was destined to go before the Lord, to be great before the Lord, and to turn many of the children of Israel to the Lord their God, was a moment of great joy. On a human level, it was her time to bask in the limelight of God's honour. But as Mary enters, there is no hint of jealousy as she gives way and owns the superior greatness of Mary and the superior greatness of the Babe in the womb. There is no sense in which she resents Mary's greater blessing as compared to hers. She readily gives way and blesses her younger relative. The secret to this lack of competitiveness is that "she was filled with the Holy Spirit" (v 41).

Many of our problems as companies of the Lord's people stem from personality conflicts and competition for place and prestige. In these early chapters of Luke, those filled with the Spirit of God are occupied with Christ and are marked by a selfless desire to glorify Him. If this marked each of us, it would result in unity and harmony instead of the endless problems which plague us. Spirit-filled believers are selfless believers. Spirit-filled believers are concerned with the honour of Christ, His place and His prestige.

Here is an older woman ministering to a younger woman, without any attitude of condescension or patronage. Paul instructed older woman to teach and encourage the younger women in areas that were not suitable for Titus to handle (Titus 2). This is still a needed ministry among believers today. The ministry of encouragement is a vital service, needed especially for those young in the faith, as well as others. Naomi encouraged Ruth, Jonathan encouraged David, and Onesiphorus encouraged Paul. Here is a ministry opened to all believers. It may not garnish headlines or mention in the magazine, but it will be recognised at the Bema.

Her Confirmation and Its Importance

"There shall be a performance of those things that were told her from the Lord" (v 45). A teenage girl faced with a pregnancy and all it entailed in 1st century Israel, would likely have lots of natural fears. Elisabeth's words would calm anxieties on two levels. First, since Elisabeth had no way of knowing of Mary's conception, it was a reassurance from the Lord of its reality and all that the angel had related. Second, it would confirm that she would carry the child to term and deliver without any complication. Few women have had this reassurance. Elisabeth's words would confirm all that the angel had said.

Her Comfort and Its Influence

Place yourself in Mary's position. She is a teenage girl who is now with child. She is unwed or at least, her marriage with Joseph had not gone beyond the betrothal period. In ancient Israel, she would be a candidate for stoning. At best, she will be a marked woman, living in shame and disgrace the remainder of her days. The godly would look down on her for her sin. The ungodly would mock her in light of her professed godliness.

How did Elisabeth receive her? She was in for a surprise. As soon as she enters, Elisabeth pronounces her "blessed" and not "cursed." Here was a godly woman, Elisabeth, who did not question the origin of this pregnancy. She, being full of the Holy Spirit, was able to recognise that the pregnancy and the child were indeed "blessed" and of God.

We can scarcely begin to appreciate the comfort and consolation this would have given to Mary. To have a godly older woman such as Elisabeth understand the circumstances of her condition must have brought great reassurance to Mary. There would be those who would gossip; there would be tongues used in reproach and mockery. But if the godly understood, what did the others matter? Mary learned that God was able to give reassurance and encouragement in the pathway of obedience and faith.

Enoch

"Two roads diverged in a wood, and I, I took the one less traveled by, and that has made all the difference."

Robert Frost

Reading: *Genesis 5:18-24; Hebrews 11:5-6; Jude 14-16*

His Uniqueness

With apologies to the American Poet, Robert Frost, Enoch travelled that road, the less travelled and less crowded one, almost four millennia ago, long before Frost penned his poem. Enoch took a road that no one else took. In that world before the flood, as iniquity was growing into a virtual tsunami to engulf the world, there was a man who was different. His name was Enoch. He chose to walk with God.

His name is found in five different places in our Bibles, two of them being in genealogies. We will dismiss these just focusing on the three that involve something about his life. They are found in:

- Genesis 5 — His Pedigree and Pathway with God
- Hebrews 11 — The Pleasure he brought to God
- Jude — The Prophecy he uttered for God

Enoch is one of the only two men of whom it is recorded that "he walked with God." The other, of course, was Noah. He walked with God despite the independence that marked the age as seen in Genesis 4, the demands and pressures of family life (5:22), the faithlessness of his generation (Heb 11), and the ungodliness of the day (Jude).

Enoch is also one of the only two men who went to heaven without dying, the other being Elijah. But there is one aspect in which Enoch stands alone. Here is the only man in Scripture (apart from the perfect Man, our Lord Jesus), of whom it was written that "he pleased God." We have many admonitions as to how we can please God. But here is a man who did please God. It is of interest that even before we read of his faithful preaching, we read in Hebrews 11 that he pleased God. I think it is safe to assume that his life of pleasing God was not due to preaching and great crowds coming and being converted. He pleased God by walking with God in a wicked world.

This should be a great encouragement to us. Our society places great emphasis on doing; in fact, your value is often determined by what you accomplish. God places greater value on what you are. When heaven was opened to proclaim God's delight in His Son, it was after 30 years of quiet living in Nazareth. He had not performed a miracle, preached a sermon, spoken a parable, or issued any decrees. It was a spotless life lived quietly in fellowship with God that brought pleasure to the heart of God.

His Distinctiveness

As you read through the "generations of Adam" given to us in Genesis 5, a recurring pattern quickly emerges and is evident.

We have a description of the person and that he lived so many years.

Then we are given the descendants – He begat

Once again we have the duration of his life – how long he lived

Finally, his death – and he died.

Description, descendants, duration, and then death: this pattern holds true. It is followed for nine of the ten men mentioned in chapter 5. But one is distinct and that very difference stands out, demanding an explanation. It is proclaiming a truth of tremendous value. When we arrive at Enoch, the seventh from Adam, we have the same initial truth concerning his life and descendants, but then we have two jarring differences. Instead of the familiar refrain that he lived so many years after begetting a son, we read that "He walked with God." And then, as though that is not enough of a distinction, instead of "and he died," we read that "he was not for God took him."

Is the Spirit of God contrasting the normal life that we live with the abundant life of "walking with God?" Is He contrasting walking with God with merely living? Here then is life as God intended it to be lived. This is the life which the Lord Jesus came to impart to all believers. Enoch, by faith, separated himself from a godless age, choosing to walk with God. The birth of his son, Methuselah, was evidently the impetus for this change, as we shall see. But the choice was still Enoch's.

The Succinctness of His Biography

In a few terse statements we are given a biography of this giant in the faith from a past age. We are told about:

The Times in which He Lived

As indicated, Genesis 4 is contemporaneous with Genesis 5. The "heroes" of the godly line in chapter 5 had to live amidst the immorality, spiritual indifference, materialism, and arrogance of the evil men of Genesis 4. That was the society in which Enoch found himself. It bears a striking resemblance to our day. While the world has not changed in one sense, it has worsened in the fact that the evil which men once perpetrated is now seen as "normal" and routine. Good has become evil and evil has become good.

The Turning Point

But Enoch's life suddenly changed with the birth of his son, Methuselah. All are familiar with the meaning of his name: "When he is dead it shall be sent (the deluge)." Enoch was aware that the world was under the judgment of God and would soon face the consequences of its sin. This so changed Enoch's perspective that it appears from that moment on, it also changed his life. From the birth of his son, with the announcement of a world under judgment, he walked with God. Enoch believed what God revealed, and thus controlled his life by something he never saw, but that he knew was coming.

Truth He Proclaimed

It is left for the next to last book of our Bible, Jude, to reveal to us that Enoch was a preacher and a prophet. He announced to his generation that God was about to judge the world. "The Lord cometh with ten thousands of His saints to execute judgment upon all …"

Enoch must have been a man of moral might and courage to proclaim a message such as this to a generation characterised by ungodly deeds and speech. No converts are recorded and certainly no plaudits were gained from his contemporaries.

Cartoons and the media lampoon the person walking the streets of the city with a sandwich board announcing the coming end of the world and its judgment. Yet, that is what marked Enoch (minus the sandwich board).

The Testimony He Obtained

Hebrews tells us that he had this testimony, "That he pleased God." We learn as well from Hebrews 11 that the principle upon which a life that is pleasing to God is based, is the principle of faith. Now lest any despair that somehow faith is only a commodity for preachers, missionaries, and elders, recall that Enoch was a family man. He lived in a difficult time. His faith grasped the fact of a coming judgment that made living for this world a futile goal and living for the next, a valuable priority. His life was based on a word from God.

In the same manner, everyone who builds his or her life according to the truth of God is living by faith and thus, pleasing God. The mother who raises her children according to the Scriptures is living by faith. The employee or employer who conducts business in keeping with the principles of Scripture is living by faith. "The just shall live by faith" is not just for salvation. Here is the truth that should control our lives.

Peter emphasised a similar truth in his second epistle. He depicts for us, as God did to Enoch, a world under judgment awaiting the stroke of God. In light of that, he wrote, "What manner of persons ought ye to be in all holy conversation and godliness" (2 Peter 3:11). This is the final motivation of the many that Peter supplied throughout his two epistles, for holy living. All that the world esteems will soon be destroyed and burnt up. Only what is of eternal value will have any value in that day!

The Translation He Experienced

In Genesis 5 we are told that "he was not, for God took him." In Hebrews 11 that "He was translated that he should not see death." Picturesque language has been employed depicting Enoch walking with God into the sunset of the day. So enjoyable was the time together that God told Enoch that, rather than returning to his home, that He would, instead, take him to His home in heaven. But I think that the words added in Hebrews 11 give a slightly different picture. "He was not found," suggests to me that the "ungodly men" of his day were looking for him, perhaps to kill him. "Not found" is actually one word which could be translated "disappeared." Certainly, the preaching as recorded in Jude would have made Enoch a very undesirable and unpopular person. If men are not able to silence the message, they will then resort to silencing the messenger.

One day they decided that they were going to put an end to his preaching. They were looking for him to take his life, but God intervened and took him away from the scene to frustrate the men of his day and perhaps, also, to confirm Enoch's testimony to them. If so, this was not only mercy to Enoch, but an act of mercy in God speaking to the men of that age by the miraculous removal of his servant.

His Usefulness

Several very encouraging truths emerge from a consideration of Enoch's life. A life marked by walking with God is open to every believer. This is not dependent on gift or intellect. Here is a privilege open to each believer. It can be enjoyed, as in Enoch's case, amidst family life and in a secular and godless society.

And what of the possibility of pleasing God? It again is open to every believer. It is predicated upon a life lived consistent with the truth of God. Principles which the world mocks become the foundation for our lives. Every step of faith in a believer's life is a step that brings pleasure to the heart of our God.

The life of Enoch also contains a reassurance as to the accuracy of Scripture. Note the following:

Enoch was 65 when Methuselah was born.

Methuselah lived 187 years and had Lamech.

Methuselah lived 782 years after Lamech

Lamech was 182 when he had Noah

Noah was 600 years old when the flood came.

Do the math: Methuselah died the year Noah entered into the ark. Maybe he died the same month, or even the same week. Scripture's accuracy is seen as we tabulate the years ascribed to each of these men in the antediluvian period.

Finally, looking at the comparative chronology of the years of the lives of the men of Genesis 5 reveals one additional fact. Aside from Abel who was murdered, the first recorded death was that of Adam. And before another man died, Enoch was translated. God, thus, teaching at the very dawn of history, that there would be two ways for believers to leave earth: either by death or by translation. God was testifying to the rapture 3,000 years before He revealed it to Paul who revealed it to us.

Enoch's life is a virtual summary of what a believer's life ought to be: walking with God, pleasing God, testifying for God, and going to be with God.

Epaphras

"Prayer should not be regarded as a duty which must be performed, but rather as a privilege to be enjoyed."

E.M. Bounds

"As is the business of tailors to make clothes and cobblers to make shoes, so it is the business of Christians to pray."

Martin Luther

Reading: *Colossians 1:3-9; 4:12-13*

The Man

We are indebted to two references in Paul's letter to the Colossians and one in Philemon for the brief yet insightful portrait we have of Epaphras. Some have confused him with the man, Epaphroditus, mentioned in the epistle to the Philippians. But they were two distinct men, one linked with Philippi and the other with Colosse in Asia Minor. Epaphras laboured in the Lycus River Valley, an area known for its hot baths and for the dye industry which had made many wealthy (Laodicea).

Just taking the main thought from each reference to the man, we find that he is described as:

- Col 1:7 - He is a Fellow servant — This expression says as much about Paul as it does about Epaphras. Paul shows no jealousy or sense of self-importance. The man who is working locally, Epaphras, is linked with the man who had a global vision, Paul. Paul does not demean him or in any manner minimise his contribution to the work of God. Epaphras is a fellow servant in the work of the Lord. Paul accords him the status which he himself had, a bondslave of Christ.

His service for the Lord was marked by sacrifice and selfless labour. His journey to Rome to acquaint Paul with the situation in Colosse is only one instance of his self-sacrificing manner.

- Col 4:12 - He is One of you, a faithful servant of Christ. Once again Paul's esteem for Epaphras and his recognition of the service he is doing for the Lord is evident. "A faithful servant of Christ" is high praise indeed, especially when coming from the praiseworthy. "One of you" is not slighting Epaphras in the least but simply identifying him as being amongst the believers in Colosse and perhaps emphasising his sphere of labour and usefulness for God. It was there at Colosse that he had proved faithful to the Lord.

- Philemon 23 - He is a Fellow-prisoner. It is possible that Epaphras chose to stay with the apostle and share his imprisonment. Paul, having sent Timothy and others away to deal with individual issues in Corinth and elsewhere, and returning Onesimus to Philemon, would need someone to minister to his daily needs. Epaphras may have volunteered to share Paul's house in which he was under house arrest. The epistle, therefore, was carried back to Colosse by Tychicus, along with Onesimus. Epaphras remained behind to serve the Lord by serving the apostle in Rome.

We know very little else about this faithful servant of the Lord. It appears he was content to labour in a small defined area, to have a close link with one assembly, Colosse, but to have a burden for neighbouring assemblies and the spiritual maturity of the believers.

It is a reminder that much of spiritual work is done by those who "stay by the stuff" and serve in a quiet and unspectacular way. No one saw his prayer life; no one likely heard the name Epaphras outside of the Lycus River Valley. He sought to be a help locally to the saints.

His Ministry

There are at least three ministries in which Epaphras was engaged. He was evidently a pioneer in the gospel. It may well be that all three assemblies in the Valley owed their beginning to him: Colosse, Laodicea, and Hierapolis.

The conclusion that he planted the assembly in Colosse is supported by Paul's description of him in chapter 1:3-8. His planting of the assemblies in Laodicea and Hierapolis is inferred from his deep exercise for their spiritual growth and for the proximity of the assemblies. He laboured as an evangelist, teacher, and possibly a shepherd to the believers in Colosse.

He was also marked out as a man with a prayer ministry – "striving fervently" in prayer for the believers. In all of these ministries he is seen as a faithful steward, one to whom the Lord had committed the welfare of the believers, and who sought to be faithful in his stewardship.

A ministry which is perhaps not at first appreciated is that his burden for the saints resulted in a communication with the apostle, resulting in the epistle we now call, the Epistle to Colosse. We are indebted to this man's discernment and burden for an epistle and its teaching that emphasises the preeminence of Christ. Think how much the poorer we would be without this incredible letter!

It is very likely that Epaphras went to Rome to speak face to face with the apostle about the doctrinal matters which were plaguing Colosse. His burden for the welfare of the saints is seen, not only in his fervent prayer for them, but in his willingness to hazard the journey to Rome. Travel in first century Europe and Asia was not only hampered by roads and vehicles (or their lack), but by the danger of thieves on the road. Just ask the man who travelled from Jerusalem down to Jericho in Luke 10.

His Manner

Two adjectives are employed by the Spirit of God to describe the character of this man's service: faithful and fervent.

His faithfulness was first of all to the person of Christ, and then to truth of God. In reality, these two cannot be separated. As false doctrine began to infiltrate the Anatolia region, Epaphras could discern that it was giving Christ a lower place, a secondary role, in Christian living. He discerned at once the disastrous consequences this would have on the believers, and the dishonour it would bring to the Lord Jesus. This led to his resolve to acquaint the apostle and to seek his help in refuting the errors.

But he was also faithful to the saints in Colosse as well as the other local assemblies. His faithfulness meant that he did not stand by and allow them to be infected with erroneous doctrine. He must act quickly to protect the saints.

All who are called to leadership in a local assembly can attest to the need for vigilance as well as discernment. New ideas and theological "fads" are constantly coming and going. Some have a siren-like quality, attracting the less stable. There are always believers looking for something more exciting or sensational. When to deal with some of these issues is always a dilemma. Many die a natural death; others linger on the periphery. But anything which touches on the person of Christ must be dealt with Biblically and quickly.

Epaphras is also credited with labouring "fervently" (I know it is an adverb and not an adjective here), in prayer. There are at least two things about his prayer life worthy of our attention: his intensity and his intelligence. "Labouring fervently" is all one word in the original Greek, and has given us our English word, "agonise." It carries the thought of striving with all one's might. He really prayed. This was not a mere recitation of his bedtime prayer. This was not a going over of his prayer list (Nothing wrong with this, in itself). He saw a need, recognised a danger, and set himself to prayer. Notice again, the combination of human responsibility – he travelled to Rome to enlist Paul's help, and divine sovereignty – he prayed fervently. The one does not negate the other. Likely, part of his prayer for the believers was that they would bow to the teaching of Paul's letter that they were about to receive. The best of ministry from the most Spirit-filled men, still needs the work of the Spirit of God as it is received by believers.

Most of us would have to confess that it takes a crisis, especially within our families, to provoke this kind of exercise in prayer. Yet, it appears that he "always" prayed this way. His deep burden for the believers and the assemblies was reflected in his prayer life.

Secondly, he displayed intelligence in prayer. "That ye may stand perfect and complete in all the will of God." This is not praying that Simeon might know whom to marry, or that Mary will be raised up from her bed of sickness, nor that Joshua might get a better job. Prayer for these daily necessities and life choices is vital and necessary. But at this crisis point, Epaphras had bigger things on his mind.

The "will of God" for which he prayed was identical to the "will of God" to which Paul alludes in his prayer for the believers (1:9). That "will" concerns His Son and God's purposes that "in all things He might have the preeminence." God's will is for His Son to have the highest place in creation and also within the Church. If I appreciate that, I will then automatically appreciate that He must have the highest place in my life. There is a very real sense, that giving Him that place in my own life will actually answer all the other issues: my career, choice of a spouse, approach to illness, and to trials.

Epaphras stands as a reminder to us all of the value of labouring for God in a local sphere, of spiritual discernment, and of fervent and intelligent prayer. May we profit from the lessons that his life affords to us.

Epaphroditus

"We have courage because we know what God is capable of doing. He does great and magnificent things. So, submit your life to Him and nothing can stand in your way."

Reading: *Philippians 2:25-30; 4:15-18*

Paul's Reasons for Writing

Paul, the prisoner, was in his own hired house under house arrest in Rome. The events leading up to this are detailed for us in the final chapters of the book of Acts. Many miles distant in Philippi, the assembly was determined to express their fellowship with Paul by sending him a gift. In 1st century Europe, this entailed a messenger who would personally carry the gift to the recipient. Considering travel conditions, this was no mean feat for anyone. A brother named Epaphroditus willingly offered to be the messenger.

Having received the gift from the assembly, Paul took pen in hand and wrote a "thank you" note to the assembly including not only thanks, but doctrinal teaching and exhortations which have been a spiritual goldmine to believers through the centuries. As well he was writing to still their fears concerning their messenger, Epaphroditus, and the news that had reached them concerning his illness. It is in these few statements which Paul makes concerning him, that we learn something of the character of this man.

The Company He Kept

He is introduced to us as "my brother, companion in labour, and fellow-soldier, and your messenger, and he that ministered to my wants" (2:25). At least five things are evident from Paul's description

He Shared in Life With Paul – Paul's Affection

He was a brother. Even before mention is made of his labour and service, his link with Paul in life in Christ is highlighted. Paul's affection for Epaphroditus is evident in the touching and gracious way he refers to him. Nowhere else does Paul employ five statements to describe another believer.

He Shared in Labour – His Activity

We are not informed as to what the nature of this labour was. Perhaps he assisted Paul by serving in some capacity during Paul's imprisonment. Perhaps Paul viewed the communication of the gift and all that Epaphroditus endured to bring it to him, as a labour.

He Shared in a Link With Paul – Adversity

Paul calls Epaphroditus a "fellow soldier." His efforts showed that he had enlisted in the great battle to further the gospel and honour the Lord. Identification with a prisoner of Rome was not a position of great honour. Suspicion could be cast upon any who befriended an enemy of the state. But Epaphroditus was willing to be linked with Paul the prisoner in his adversity.

His Loyalty to the Stewardship – His Association With the Saints

He had been handed a responsibility as a messenger from the assembly in Philippi and had completed it at great cost. He represented the assembly and did it faithfully. It is likely that the gifts sent included not only money but supplies and necessities which Paul would need during his house arrest. Nothing was supplied by Rome to prisoners. All had to be brought by family or friends.

His Love for Paul – His Administration

He is recorded as having "publicly ministered to my wants" (Margin, Newb. v 25). Paul had a high view of the service that this faithful servant of Christ had rendered. Epaphroditus took the place of a humble servant, serving the needs of the apostle. He employs language which almost suggests a priestly or Levitical form of service to Paul.

The Confidence Bestowed in Him

Maybe it was at a "business meeting" or some similar informal gathering of the believers. Everyone agreed that it was imperative to forward a gift to the apostle Paul. But how to get the gift to Rome was the matter now under discussion. It was a journey of perhaps 800 miles. Roads were not only rudimentary but dangerous. Robbers frequented the road and travel was far from safe. Who would go? Perhaps it was from some quiet corner of the room that a willing voice was heard: "Here am I. Send me." It was, of course, Epaphroditus. He was willing to face the challenge and sacrifice of making the journey. Am I available for God to use? Is my life so busy and my schedule so full that God could not entrust me with a mission for His glory?

Conversely, do others have the confidence in me that is essential to enable them to entrust me with a work for God? The confidence displayed in Epaphroditus was not the result of a day or two of service, but the result of years of observing a man who was faithful with everything that was placed in his hands. If you would like responsibility in God's assembly, do at this present moment whatever God has entrusted to you, and do it to the very best of your ability. It is required in a steward "that a man be found faithful" (1 Cor 4:2).

The Concerns He Had

One of the features which marked the Lord Jesus in His selfless Servant character was that He esteemed others better than Himself

(2:3). This, of course, is not a reference to inherent personhood but to a priority of concern. Such was the estimation of the Son, that He chose to put our welfare ahead of His own, resulting in a cross death.

It is then with a sense of, "I just read that earlier in the chapter," that we note that Epaphroditus put the concern and welfare of the believers in his home assembly ahead of his own. News had filtered back to the believers at Philippi, that Epaphroditus' journey had resulted in sickness so severe, that he was close to death. Given the primitive communication system of the 1st century, this would suggest that the illness may have been protracted. Having heard of their concern for him, Epaphroditus was "full of heaviness" or sorrow. He was more concerned with the welfare of the believers than with his own state of health.

Most of us would have been thankful if others were aware of our sacrifice and costly service, but not Epaphroditus. He was not looking for glory or sympathy for his service.

The Commitment He Showed

We are not told of the route which he took to the visit the apostle in Rome. Was it by land and sea or totally over land? Either way, a minimum would be a distance of 800 miles. This was accomplished with none of the conveniences which we enjoy today. Somewhere during his journey or at Rome, he fell ill. It would seem from the wording that it was on the way to accomplish his service. Facing the danger of the possibility that his journey could cost his life he made a choice. "Not regarding his life" almost suggests that he gambled with his life. He decided to pursue his goal despite the risk entailed. It was a conscious choice to accomplish his goal at the cost of his life.

While everything truly given to the Lord has the character of an offering, perhaps it is this added "offering" of Epaphroditus' life which leads Paul to use the lofty language of chapter 4. The gift which was sent by the assembly to Paul is referred to as "an odour of a sweet smell, a sacrifice acceptable, well pleasing to God" (v 18). God received a reminder of His Son in the gift which was sent from the assembly and administered by Epaphroditus.

The Commendation He Received

He was to be held in "reputation" or honour for the service he performed and for the dangers he had encountered. Paul urges this recognition not only because of the material blessing he had received from his hand, but for the selfless consecration which appeared to mark his service. Not only what he had done, but how he did it and why he persevered, are all reasons for lauding this faithful servant. If the valued but imperfect assessment of the apostle is so honouring, what will the assessment at the Bema be for each of us? There, it will not be a flawed biased human judge, but the righteous Judge of all the earth.

The Conformity He Displayed

We have all heard and enjoyed ministry which has detailed how the example of the Perfect Servant in Philippians 2:5-8 was emulated by the three servants who follow: Paul, Timothy, and Epaphroditus. Now allow me to underline a few details in the latter's history that magnify this for us.

He was sent with a work to accomplish; he traveled a great distance from his home; it brought him to the very point of death, as he did not consider his own life in light of the work given him to accomplish. Then we read that God in mercy intervened and raised him up. Next he is being returned to his native sphere, and he is to be held in honour. Notice: devotion to a work, death, raised up, returned, receiving honour. All of these steps mirror something of the steps of the perfect Servant earlier in the chapter. Epaphroditus' illness enabled him to be brought into a greater conformity to Christ. We need to be often reminded that the "good" to which all things are working (Rom 8:28), is moral conformity to the Lord Jesus. All of life's circumstances are intended to be for our spiritual blessing and growth. The manner in which we respond to them will determine their ultimate fruitfulness in each of our lives.

The Consequences

Consider the consequences of that of which we have been writing.

Paul's needs were met. This in itself was no small accomplishment. This enabled the apostle to continue his written ministry while in Rome and to await his eventual release. Then, the assembly had this "fruit" placed in the ledger of heaven under their account.

Also, the Father was reminded in the gift of the self-sacrificing gift of His Son. The "giving" of the saints combined with the conscious choice of the giving of his life if necessary by their minister, was an echo of the "mind of Christ" (v 5).

We have, also, an epistle from the pen of the apostle which has a wealth of teaching for us and one of the greatest Christological "hymns" found in the epistles. Has a Breaking of Bread ever occurred without some reference to or citation of Philippians 2:5-8?

Finally, there is the process by which God was bringing Epaphroditus into greater conformity to Christ. The stewardship of the gift, the conscious choice to lay down his life if needed, and the concern for others instead of self, all were the fruit of the experiences through which he passed. Epaphroditus has left us a standard for faithfulness and selfless service, inscribed on the pages of Scripture for time and eternity.

Gaius

"Adversity is the diamond dust Heaven polishes its jewels with."

Thomas Carlyle

Reading: *3 John*

Your lexicon will suggest that there were several different men in the New Testament who bore the name of Gaius. It is tempting to link the Gaius of 3rd John with the Gaius of Macedonia or of Corinth, but we will confine our remarks to the Gaius who appears in 3rd John and his story as unfolded by John. Certainly, there are an abundance of lessons for our spiritual profit found in just these 14 verses.

His Situation

Gaius was part of an assembly in which a domineering leader made life difficult. Diotrephes was an autocratic bully, a one-man wrecking crew, and a despotic ruler. Intimidation, arrogance, and unscriptural policies in relation to reception and excommunication marked his tenure in the assembly. Even his salvation is called into question, after John, having provided Demetrius as a good example to follow, seems to contrast him with Diotrephes, and then says, "follow not that which is evil" (v 11). The sovereignty of God had allowed Gaius to be exposed to this harsh leadership. So great was the burden on this younger man, that it may well have affected his health (v 2). To both John and Gaius' credit, there was no suggestion of rebellion, no hint that Gaius should withdraw and begin another assembly. He was encouraged by the apostle, as we shall note, to do what he could for the Lord where he was.

In a day when there was not the plethora of options for someone who leaves an assembly, there was only one place for a believer despite the difficulties, and that was in a local assembly. Many chafe under the perceived difficulties of being part of an assembly where they feel that their gift is not recognised, or their contributions not appreciated. Gaius did not labour under any imaginary limitations. It was all very real and literal in his case. Yet his response to these issues is what is so noteworthy.

His Commendation

I seriously doubt if John, guided by the Spirit of God, stoops to flattery. His commendation of Gaius is effusive, and no doubt merited. There was first of all:

The Principle That Controlled His Walk

John describes Gaius as one marked by, "the truth that is in thee, even as thou walkest in the truth" (v 3). This unique description reveals what was the guiding principle in his life. The Word of God controlled every choice and decision which he confronted. It is important to recognise that "truth" or "doctrine" is always in the singular. Jude spoke and wrote of "the truth once for all delivered to the saints." The unity of truth is in itself, a vital "truth" to grasp. We do not hold a number of disparate doctrines. All truth holds together as all relates ultimately to the person, work, and glory of Christ. We cannot pick and choose, discarding what we find difficult to live out or practice. Compromising one aspect of truth ultimately compromises all the truth.

The Priority That Controlled His Actions

The great priority of his life was the honour of the Lord Jesus. His exercise was to be of help to those who were moving amongst the people of God, the strangers, and brethren of verse 5. This was being done for the honour of the Name of the Lord Jesus. They had gone forth taking "nothing of the Gentiles for His Name's sake." Identifying with them in their exercise, Gaius was also expressing his desire to honour that Name. As such, he has now earned the title of a "fellow-helper of the truth."

The Practice That Marked His Life

We are told that what he did, he did "after a godly sort." There are several ways of understanding this phrase. Each of them raises the service of Gaius to a very high level. Each challenges us in our service for the Lord.

One way of understanding this phrase is that he was doing it as God Himself would do it. At the very least it would suggest that nothing was held back. Generosity and copiousness would have marked his care for the believers. Whatever needs they had, financial, material, emotional, or simply information – all were readily supplied. Here was a man on earth expressing, by his actions, the heart of God in heaven! Gaius did this by hospitality. This is a service still needed and valued amongst us today.

The phrase might also be understood that he did it "worthy of God." This is a more literal translation. The concept behind the word "worthy" is the idea of something equal or balanced. It is a word which Paul employs on a number of occasions. His estimation of God was equaled by his care for these visitors. He was able to express his love and devotion to the Lord by his treatment of His people. We are reminded of Abraham who entertained visitors (Gen 18) and was able to show hospitality to the Divine Visitor, giving Him his very best.

The Lord Jesus seems to link together love for His person with the feeding and care of the lambs and the sheep in His encounter with Peter by Tiberias (John 21). While absolute purity of motive is an elusive goal while in our bodies, the more an action springs from love to Christ, the closer it gets to being selfless and pure.

A final way of appreciating the phrase is that he was doing it as though he were doing it unto the Lord Himself. While that translation may not have the strongest support, the truth is supported by the Lord's words, "Inasmuch as ye have done it unto one of the least of these My brethren, ye have done it unto Me" (Matt 25:40). If we viewed our relationships and ministry in this light, it would revolutionise our treatment one of another.

Our service for the Lord should combine elements of all three of these interpretations. Service ought to be rendered out of love and devotion to the Lord. It ought to be done with the same grace and bounty that God would do it. And it should be done as though we were doing it to Him, personally.

Maturation

Gaius is held up for generations which succeed him as an example of someone marked by soul prosperity (v 2). Yet, this prosperity of soul occurred in very unusual soil. The assembly where he was found was not one that was marked by warm and happy fellowship and rich ministry. He grew in difficult circumstances; nothing was conducive to growth. It is a reminder that spiritual growth can never be hindered by those who oppose us. Joseph grew in his parent's house, Potiphar's house, the prison house, and Pharaoh's house. Whether the hatred of his brothers, the demands of a busy administration, the cruel chains that "entered into his soul" (Ps 105:18), or the pressure of the public eye, he was able to enjoy the presence of God and to give pleasure to God. John the Baptist grew in the wilderness until the days of his public ministry to the nation. And the Lord Jesus increased in all His ways as a child in Nazareth (Luke 2:51, 52).

Spiritual growth is an area open to all believers regardless of the circumstances into which the will of God brings them. The very circumstances that we may complain are a hindrance to growth may well be the ones designed by God to foster our growth. The grace of God will always meet us wherever the will of God places us.

Inspiration

The Scriptures, and even the lives of fellow believers, provide examples that should encourage us. We must always remember that the godly lives and accomplishment of the heroes of the faith were not given to us to try and imitate, nor to intimidate. They are given to inspire us in our own lives. If they could live for God amidst their circumstances, with the Lord's help, we can as well.

To encourage Gaius, John draws his attention to a man named Demetrius. We know nothing of him apart from this one verse from John's pen. Yet he was a man worth emulating or at the least, from whom he could draw encouragement. We are told that he had the universal witness of all, the uncompromising witness of the truth of God, and the unassailable witness of the apostle. Here was a man to whom Gaius could look for inspiration in his desire to live to please God.

There are rare instances when a man must go it alone – no encouragement outside the Lord, no fellowship outside of the divine. Normally, however, God will supply encouragement and even fellowship for those seeking to live a life that pleases Him: Elijah will have his Elisha, Paul his Timothy, Moses his Joshua.

May we be like Gaius, and be able to grow and serve in whatever circumstances the will of God places us. May we also be men and women such as Demetrius who can serve as role models and sources of encouragement to other believers.

Hagar

"No one but God her need could meet,
Show her in pity for her boy
A well of water at her feet
That filled her broken heart with joy."

I.Y. Ewan

Reading: *Genesis 16:1-11; 21:9-20*

Our Interpretation

If we are going to profit from the life of Hagar, the Egyptian handmaid, we need to alter our thinking. We need to move from the typical and dispensational, to the personal. What I mean is that if we view Hagar in light of Galatians 4, we will only see her in a negative light. She is the bondwoman who, with her son, must be cast out to make room for the son of the free. Law must give way to grace.

If, however, we view her personally, there are other and valuable lessons to learn. This shift from the typical or corporate to the individual is not something unknown in Scripture. For example, we see all of Israel redeemed from Egypt by the blood of the lamb at Passover. Yet we read that many of them perished (individually) in the wilderness due to unbelief (Heb 3 and 4). If we only think in terms of the typical picture and the corporate, we will think that everyone was "saved" in N. T. language. Yet the teaching of the book of Numbers, as well as those chapters cited in Hebrews, tells us otherwise.

Now back to Hagar as a person and individual, and her life and lessons.

Deviations and Their Fruit

Abram had lived 10 years in the land, all the while waiting for the promise of God to be fulfilled. If there was one person who could expect that his marriage would be blessed with an heir, it was Abram. God had promised this to him (Gen 15). But as time passed, patience gave way to expediency.

Sarai (as she was then called), takes the lead. Here is deviation number one. Rather than being a help and support to Abram in his trial, she becomes a source of error. She suggests a shortcut to God's plan. Deviation number two follows swiftly as leadership passes from Abram to his wife, and Abram follows the lead of his wife. Genesis is actually a study in failed leadership, beginning with Adam in Genesis 3.

Sarai suggests that Abram should take Hagar her maid, recently brought out of Egypt, and conceive a child through her. Hagar becomes a second wife (v 3) to Abram and Hagar quickly conceives and bears Abram a son, Ishmael.

As a result, Sarai "was despised in (Hagar's) her eyes." This means that Hagar would look on Sarai as the cause of the infertile marriage and look down on her. Infertility was a reproach in that culture (Luke 1:25). Hagar, here, gets low marks for her attitude toward her mistress. While the Word of God does not advocate slavery as a lifestyle, it does promote respect and honour to those above us in position. Her insubordination leads Sarai to realise her mistake and she now chides Abram for the result. Consequently, Abram turns the disposing of the matter over to his wife who "dealt hardly" with Hagar.

Fast forward another 14 years and now Sarah has given birth to Isaac. The feast is held at the time of weaning and as a result of Ishmael's mockery of Isaac, Sarah insists that Hagar and Ishmael must be turned out. Though once again taking the lead in decisions within the home, the Lord ratifies her demand and, with great reluctance, Abraham sends them away (21:14). When the water and bread were spent, she despairs of life, lifting her voice with weeping.

Once again the Angel of Lord calls to her and provides both a promise of a future for the child, and provision for the way. Her eyes are opened, and she sees a well of water. The curtain closes on her life by telling us that God was with the lad as he grew in the wilderness. His mother, an Egyptian, took him a wife from Egypt. Ishmael will become a great nation. Typology is fulfilled (Gal 4) and her personal history concluded.

Revelation

God cares for an Egyptian slave girl! He sees her circumstances, the abuse she is receiving, the danger of her condition, the anxiety for her son – He sees all this and more. His compassions are evident in His dealing with Hagar. At His first encounter in Genesis 16, His pointed question as to her destination makes clear that she cannot go much farther. He has a care for her. He names her expected son, suggesting a destiny and purpose for him, then assures her that "the Lord hath heard her affliction."

Her response, "Thou God seest me," has been variously translated. Some suggest that it should read "You are a God Who sees me" or something similar. Open to even more divergent translations is what follows. "Have I also looked after Him that seeth me?" "Have I remained alive here after seeing Him?" (NASB). I prefer the thought that she is moved to think that the God Whom she never sought, has been seeking her. She is overwhelmed at the mercy and goodness of God. Would you allow this as her conversion?

Genesis 21 is the final encounter we have recorded of Hagar and the Lord. Now once again heaven is attentive to her needs, calms her fears, opens her eyes, and shows her a well of water. Then there is the assurance given concerning the lad (Ishmael). His future is assured, and God promises to make of him a great nation.

To this Egyptian slave, God has revealed Himself as omniscient, kind and compassionate, sovereign and sensitive, merciful and gracious. Although Sarah did not reveal God to Hagar by her actions, God revealed Himself to her in a Theophany and in a message from heaven. She responded to the revelation and lived in the good of it.

Implications of Law of First Mention

Hagar fled from the cruel treatment she was receiving from Sarai. She is found by the Angel of the Lord as she rests by a fountain on the way to Shur. The message from the Angel is "return ... submit." This is the first mention of the word "submit" in our Bible. Being the first mention, it is worthy of our attention.

The first matter is to discern Who the Angel of the Lord is? Is this one of the angels who stand before the throne? The fact that the angel is designated, "The Angel of the Lord," gives ground for identifying this as none other than the pre-incarnate Christ, the messenger from Jehovah.

For those who object to any thought of a pre-incarnate appearance of the Son of God, please bear with me as the final lesson will not be lost despite our divergent views.

It is intriguing that the first recorded words from One Who comes as a messenger from the presence of Jehovah are, "Return ... submit." We are not told when, but at some distant past time in history, there were angelic beings, led by Lucifer, who refused to submit. They rebelled and were cast out in their rebellion. They had the inestimable privilege of moving before the sapphire throne and seeing something of the ineffable glory which those cherubim in Isaiah 6 beheld. Yet, despite privilege and place, they refused to submit. God is vitally invested in the concept of submission; the Son Himself took a place of submission to accomplish redemption (1 Cor 11:3, 4).

In that same chapter, we are told that women ought to have a "sign of authority" on their heads because of the angels (v 10). Are angels learning by beholding women who willing and intelligently take a place of submission in the local church? God has decreed that submission be showcased in this way when the church meets together.

Hagar was being sent back to harsh conditions under which she would have to serve. Yet the consciousness of the eye of God upon her would serve to enable her to submit despite the difficult position in which she was found.

God intends submission at every level: government, assembly, marriage, and family life. As in the case of Hagar, it is not always pleasant and easy. But it is God honouring.

A similar first mention of the word "submit" in the N. T. puts its meaning beyond all doubt. "He went down with them and came to Nazareth and was subject unto them" (Luke 2:51). This memorable sentence is the finishing touch to the incident when our Lord Jesus aa boy of 12 was found in the temple. After the unjustified reprimand from His parents, He returns to Nazareth and is subject to them: the omniscient one to peasants; the creator to the carpenter, the Holy to the natural. Any suggestion that submission implies inferiority of personhood must be rejected in light of this. Divine order does not touch on the value of the person, but on the role that has been divinely given.

Application to Us

Are there lessons from which can profit in the life of Hagar? Since all the Word of God is profitable, we can assume that lessons are available for us from which we can learn.

- Failure in leadership as seen in Abram following Sari's counsel always leads to problems and confusion.

- Submission is always something which pleases God.

- The Character of God as discovered by Hagar.

Hushai, David's Friend

"A friend is someone who walks in when everyone else walks out"

Reading: *2 Samuel 15:32-37; 16:16-19*

The Commitment of a Friend

Events were unfolding with alarming, almost dizzying speed. The conspiracy that had been planned for months, or possibly even years, had been successful. Absalom had gathered much of the nation behind him, and he was about to invade the city and claim the throne. His personality and manipulative skills had engendered a dissatisfaction in the nation with David.

Now, flushed with power and driven by his own ego, Absalom was not going to let anything stand in his way or cause him to show mercy to anyone. David was faced with the choice of staying and defending the city with the possible loss of many innocent lives, or of fleeing and becoming vulnerable in the wilderness. True to his shepherd heart, David chose to sacrifice his own safety for the welfare of the people.

With haste, David, his household, the Cherethites and Pelethites, and the 600 faithful and devoted men who were with him at Gath, fled the city. The superscription to Psalm 3 indicates that it was written on this occasion. The likelihood is that Psalm 4 was also penned at this time as both Psalms breathe the same atmosphere. In Psalm 3 David cried to God, "Save me, Oh my God" (v 7). It contains, as does Psalm 4, numerous allusions to his confidence in God and his vindication. In answer to his cry, God sent at least three men to encourage David: Ittai the Gittite, Zadok the priest, and Hushai, David's friend. Ittai came with a pledge of devotion; Zadok came with the ark, the presence of God; but Hushai came to offer himself. He literally "came in when everyone else walked out."

David had said in Psalm 3, "I laid me down and slept. I awaked for the Lord sustained me" (v 5). In Psalm 4, "I will both lay me down in peace and sleep. For Thou, Lord, only makest me dwell in safety" (Ps 4:9). Yet that night was one of potential danger and catastrophic loss. Ahithophel was planning on an immediate attack which would have found David unprepared and vulnerable. In the coming of Hushai, God will provide the safety for that night's rest as we shall see.

Also notice that in 2 Samuel 15:21, David utters another prayer as he ascends Olivet weeping. "Oh Lord, I pray Thee, turn the counsel of Ahithophel into foolishness." This was no small request as the counsel of Ahithophel is likened to "as if a man had inquired at the oracle of God" (16:23).

God not only answered that prayer, but answered almost immediately. For the very next event in chapter 15, after David's prayer and worship (v 32), was the arrival of Hushai. God was providing in the man, the answer to how the counsel of Ahithophel would be frustrated.

The Cost of Friendship

David, recognising the value of Hushai and his wisdom, directed him to return to the city and to feign allegiance to Absalom. In this manner, he might be able to defeat the counsel of Ahithophel and procure for David the time he needed to be able to defend himself and his family. Some will begin to debate the issue of ethics and lying, pointing to Hushai's words to Absalom. Perhaps Hushai really did not lie. When he proclaimed, "God save the king" (16:16), he might well have had David in mind. That was what he was doing in the court of Absalom, seeking to save David, the true king.

Leaving the issue of ethics and morality aside, Hushai was placing his life on the line for David. To have been discovered as a secret agent of David's, infiltrating the court of Absalom, would have meant certain death. Absalom was not above taking lives to accomplish his ends. Hushai was willing to give his life for his friend. Though not as great a sacrifice, it does foreshadow another Who said, "Greater love hath no man than this, that man lay down his life for his friends" (John 15:13).

In our day, friendship normally does not entail sacrificing our lives (though it may in some countries). But what am I willing to sacrifice to display genuine Christian friendship? If responding to the needs of another disrupts my plans for the day, will I make that sacrifice? If it involves financial cost to me, will I make that sacrifice? Do the numerous imperatives of friendship, the "one-another" statements in the epistle, cost me anything to fulfil?

The Consequences of Faithful Friendship

It was mentioned earlier that David was able to lie down and enjoy a good night's sleep, confident that God would overrule and prevent a night-time attack. How did God accomplish this? Enter Hushai. Absalom asked for counsel from both Ahithophel and Hushai. Ahithophel counselled an immediate pursuit and attack on David. Hushai counselled otherwise. His counsel was to wait, gather all the armies together, and then go forth to do battle. Perhaps here he was appealing to Absalom's ego: the new king riding triumphantly out to battle leading the combined forces of the nation! Absalom chose to follow Hushai's battle plan instead of Ahithophel's. This bought David the time he needed. Thus, the very night when Ahithophel counselled to attack David, unknown to David God was using Hushai to defeat the counsel that was being given and to afford David time to regroup and prepare for battle. So, David was able to sleep, confident in the ability of God to protect him; and God was able to defeat the counsel of Ahithophel. The latter, realising the folly of Absalom's decision and foreseeing the defeat it guaranteed, took his own life, rather than die by the sword of David. His hatred for David was likely the result of the dishonour which David had done to one of his kinfolk and family, Bathsheba, who was probably the granddaughter of Ahithophel. But his revenge was frustrated and unfulfilled.

The Compensation of Friendship

David was victorious in the battle and the day came when he returned to the city of Jerusalem. The day of victory and vindication was accompanied by compensation for all who followed David. Barzillai was content with a kiss from the king (2 Sam 19:39). Mephibosheth was content with the presence of the king (19:30). But what of Hushai? We do not read of him again. No mention is made of his reward; no honour was bestowed upon him. And yet, is it not honour enough that three times he is known as David's friend (15:37; 16:16, 17)?

There is certainly nothing unscriptural about serving for reward. Our rewards will be linked with our worship (Rev 4:10) and will be related to our roles in the coming kingdom and eternal service for the Lord Jesus (2 Pet 1:11). But to be known eternally as a "friend of the King" would be an honour not to be despised or shunned.

Would it not be worth serving a life-time for a kiss from the King? And to be known eternally as a "friend of the King"? We sing, "How will recompense His smile, the suffering of this little while." Most of us sing this with a sense of embarrassment as we know so little of suffering. But the truth is nevertheless worth enjoying. His presence will be a reward and compensation in itself.

The Commemoration of Friendship

Is it possible that when Solomon penned his Proverbs, and when he dwelt on the value of friendship, he had Hushai in mind? He was among those of David's household who had to flee in the Absalom rebellion. He would have been among those who saw Hushai when he came to David. He likely knew and understood the value of Hushai and his counsel. As a result, he saw the value of true friendship.

He spoke of a friend loving at all seasons (Pro 17:7, 8). He spoke of a true friend being closer than a brother (18:24). He urged his son not to forsake his friend in times of need (27:10). His Proverbs contain warnings about the fickleness of friends and how easily monetary considerations and personal gain can play into such friendships (14:20;

18:4, 6, 7). And he reminded his son of how a friend can encourage by his very presence (27:9). He had witnessed all this in Hushai, David's friend.

Hushai proved to be a true friend in every sense of the word. He took his place with a rejected man, knowing it might cost him his life. His was not a friendship based upon material gain or place. It was love for his friend.

We, also, as believers have the privilege of displaying our love for a rejected Man. It may not advance us in the society in which we live nor gain us honour among men. While it may not cost us our lives, it may well cost us in earthly terms. Also, as fellow believers we can show the genuineness of our "friendship" with other saints by our sensitivity to their needs: emotional, material, and spiritual. May we, like Hushai, be known as "David's friend."

Ittai the Gittite

"One loyal friend is worth ten thousand relatives"

Euripides

Reading: *2 Samuel 15:17-22*

I know many men named David. I know quite a few, as well, named Jonathan. There are also a few Nathans in the mix and the occasional Ira. If my memory is really challenged I might even remember an Abner and Uriah. But I have never heard of anyone named Ittai. If you Google it, you will find that he does not register very high in the "most common name of the year" contest. Factor in, also, that there are perhaps six verses that deal with the life of Ittai out of the 31,102 verses in the Bible (.00016% for those of you given to numbers), and his minor role is established beyond question.

While his appearance on the page of Scripture is very brief yet what he supplied to King David is beyond our ability to assess for its worth. Also, what he has established as the standard of true loyalty is a challenge to each of us. Consider first of all:

The Crisis in the Kingdom

A rebel had seized the throne. It was a perfectly planned and executed coup. Absalom had stolen the hearts of the men of Israel. By deceit and wily diplomacy, he had succeeded in winning most of Israel to his camp. He had with him the chief counsellor, Ahithophel, and some of the best soldiers including Abner. Things did not look very hopeful for David.

But what made the situation even more dire and tragic, is that the rebel was David's own son. It was not a foreign invader who had secured the throne, but a son from his own loins. While on the one hand the government of God was operating in all of this, yet the rebellious and ambitious heart of Absalom was being displayed. It was clear that Absalom wanted not only the throne, but David's life.

Place yourself in David's situation for a moment. Someone in your own family has risen up and rebelled against you; he has shown his animosity and hostility, not only in what he has done, but in the contempt he displayed in doing it. If you did not feel some measure of abandonment, you would be a unique father. A lonely and dejected David made his way out of the city, through the valley approaching the brook Kidron, the very place where another rejected King would one day cross (John 18:1).

All this reminds us that we also live in a day of crisis. A usurper reigns in the hearts of men in our secular society. Mankind has turned its collective back on its true God and pledged it allegiance to a rebel and a rival. It is a day of crisis for us. Crisis always tests commitment! For Ittai, the crisis is about to reveal his loyalty.

The Challenge

The only feasible recourse for David was to leave the city to avoid a blood-bath. As David fled that day, the household servants and his family went with him. His personal guard, the Cherethites and the Pelethites, accompanied him. What followed must have come as a surprise to David. Six hundred men from Gath, led by Ittai the Gittite (from Gath) marched behind the Pelethites. We are not privy to what led these men to follow David. He had been at Gath back in 1 Samuel 27, a number of years earlier (not exactly one of David's finest moments). Had they seen the character of the man despite his failure? Did they recognise that here was God's anointed King? For whatever reason, Ittai and these 600 Philistines had chosen to follow David.

As David reviewed the troops who are following him, he is surprised to find Ittai and his 600 men. To him, David issues a challenge. Was it a test of loyalty? Was it a sincere request?

"Wherefore goest thou also with us? Return to thy place and abide with the king. For thou art a stranger and also an exile ... thou camest but yesterday" (2 Sam 15:19, 20). Notice several facts about this man. He was not an Israelite but a Philistine. He was not only a Philistine but from Gath the home of the giant. I can imagine that Goliath would have been a hero back in Gath before he met David. Young boys, probably Ittai among them, would have looked upon Goliath as their hero, a role model they all desired to grow up and emulate. But then news came that a young stripling, David, had defeated their champion. David spoke of his recent arrival in Israel, an exile and a stranger. We would think of him as a recent convert to David.

Ittai overcame national boundaries in following David. There were personal feelings that might have hindered but did not. Then there was the inconvenience of a new follower of David uprooting himself and his family once again. Finally, there was the spectre of certain death should Absalom's coup prove successful.

David's challenge was repeated and expanded by the One Greater than David when He issued His terms of discipleship: "If any man will come after Me, let him deny himself, and take up his cross daily, and follow Me" (Luke 9:23). Later in the chapter (vv 27-32), men who allegedly wanted to follow Christ were confronted with choices. The path that discipleship required revealed three barriers. Someone has well-characterised these men as "Mr. too hasty, Mr. too hesitant, and Mr. too homebound."

The test of discipleship comes to every believer at some crisis point in life. That crisis will reveal what really matters to us in life. We tend to prioritise family, careers, leisure, financial security, and self-interests, thus failing the test of discipleship. Ittai was faced with the choice in his day as the challenge came from David: "Return."

The Choice and the Commitment

Ittai's response was clear and unequivocal. "As my lord the king liveth, surely in what place my lord the king shall be, whether in death or life, even there will thy servant be" (v 21). There was no hesitation; there were no conditions or hints of limitations. He was "all out" for David. Can you measure what it must have meant to David for Ittai to address David as "my lord the king"? One from David's own family was attempting to wrest the crown from his head, yet here was a Gentile, a Philistine, who was owning David as king. In the day of David's rejection, a man was crowning him in his heart as the rightful king and occupant of the throne. God in His mercy provided this encouragement for David, encouragement from words that exceeded the value of 600 soldiers from Gath.

It is evident that Ittai had counted the cost. He spoke of "death and life," not "life and death." He recognised that death was the greater likelihood, but insisted on going forward with David. It took the rebellion of Absalom to reveal the depth of Ittai's devotion.

Ittai's words are almost an echo of those uttered by Ruth the Moabitess over two centuries earlier, when she was tested by Naomi. She also refused to be dissuaded by the bleak prospects that the future held for her. She would also be buried where Naomi was buried.

These examples of true devotion, these O. T. standards of loyalty, test our superficial commitment to spiritual things. In a day of materialism and prosperity, we quickly become acclimatised to a life-style which is not conducive to sacrificial discipleship. Believers must rise above numerous hindrances and barriers to live a committed life.

The Lord is not asking us to go to the martyr's stake or to bury our lives in some far off distant land (although He might), He would like to see us at all the meetings of the assembly, or seeking to develop our usefulness in the assembly, and of faithfulness to His Name. Commitment is lived out in the everyday of life, its routine and its demands.

Consequences

David acquiesced and said, "Go and pass over" (v 22). Then we read that Ittai indeed did pass over, "and all his men and all the little ones that were with him." His commitment and choice had an influence on the men who followed him, but also on his family. The little ones followed their father. We are all acutely aware that we cannot "save" our children or grandchildren. What we can do is to is to provide for them an example of commitment to eternal things, to spiritual values.

Your example of consistency and commitment may stir others to a similar choice, just as Ittai influenced his 600 men. Most of us can look back on those whose lives helped to shape ours. What we remember most was not their spiritual gifts, but their lives and what marked them (Heb 13:7). Younger believers especially are watching you and many are moulding their lives after your example.

There is one final mention of Ittai in 2 Samuel 18:2. David needed a general to whom he could commit a third of the army. He remembered a man who had committed himself to David. Such a man was fit to have David commit the army to him. The man who had faithfully followed David was the kind of man who would prove faithful in battle for David.

We are reminded that life has consequences. We are living now in light of an "abundant entrance" into the everlasting kingdom. As Mervyn Paul termed it several generations back, this is "training time for the reigning time." Faithfulness to the Lord now will result in responsibility in His eternal kingdom. Ittai knew promotion as a result of his loyalty to David. We read no more of Ittai in the sacred record. What happened when David returned and once again claimed the throne and the crown? We are not told. But one cannot help but think that Ittai was held in honour and served in David's kingdom for the remainder of his days.

He wept with David when David crossed over the brook Kidron (2 Sam 15:23); he must have rejoiced when David ascended the throne once again. Loyalty to his lord, led to honour from David's hand.

Jehoiada and Jehosheba

Not all stories end with a "happily ever after"

Selected

Reading: *2 Kings 11*

The godly in Israel must have gathered together and wept. It was a sad day. It seemed as though God's covenant with David had just been rendered invalid. Word from the palace was that all the royal seed had been destroyed. Athaliah, on hearing that her son Ahaziah had been slain, had all the sons of Ahaziah slain (her grandsons) and claimed the throne for herself. How could all this have happened? Had God failed?

The Error of One Compromise

To begin to piece together all the threads of the story we have to return to King Jehoshaphat of Judah. Jehoshaphat was a good king. The inspired writer details that he walked in the ways of David his father (2 Chron 17:3-12). That is high praise only recorded of four kings. Yet he had a major flaw – he could not say "no." As a result he entered into some very dangerous alliances. He had linked his son with a daughter of Ahab and Jezebel from Israel (1 Kings 22:4, 44). The worship of Baal marked that kingdom and was sure to infect Judah. Perhaps there is this small consolation in his action, that even a good man can make a mistake. But it was not much consolation or comfort for the people of Judah when that daughter of Ahab, Athaliah, murdered the seed royal.

Scripture repeatedly warns us both by clear precept and by tragic pictures of the danger that results from compromises and unequal alliances. Abram, Lot, David at Gath, Solomon, and others all shout to us to avoid the traps into which they fell. What may appear as a minor "concession" can lead to a major problem for a believer, a family, or an assembly.

The Evil of One Woman

Athaliah was the daughter of Ahab and Jezebel. She inherited Baal worship from her father and an ambitious, sinister, and devious mind from her mother. The DNA of her parents ran true in her. She introduced Baal worship into the southern kingdom. And when the opportunity arose, she claimed the throne and ruled for six years.

It would appear that she did not even pay lip-service to the God of Israel as she did not venture into the House of God where a rival was being secreted. She introduced all the evils of Israel into Judah. She had displaced God and God's rightful heir to the throne. It was a day of spiritual anarchy and idolatry.

She was almost successful in terminating the royal line of David. One sinner did much evil! No doubt, behind her selfish ambition was the sinister arm of Satan in his vain attempt to thwart the coming of the Messiah.

The Exercise of One Woman

We are introduced to one of the unsung heroines of Scripture. God is sovereign and will maintain His covenant with David and with the world. He will, however, use believers to fulfil that sovereign will. Jehosheba took her nephew, Joash, the only remaining heir to the throne, and was able to prevent his death. She rescued him from the cruel designs of Athaliah, without her being aware of it. She then hid him for six years in the House of the Lord. The importance of what she did is impossible to measure.

Recognising the emergency and the peril in which divine purposes suddenly hung, she moved swiftly and secured the child, hiding him and his nurse from the eyes of Athaliah. It is thrilling to see that although the entire future of God's plan for humanity hung by a slender thread, it was as secure in the hand of God as it could possibly be.

It is interesting that God used Pharaoh's daughter to save Moses; Mary and Joseph to shelter the child Jesus from Herod. Here he will employ an aunt to protect the link to the royal line through David. He has overcome the wicked plots of Haman, Hitler, Herod, Hussein, and their ilk. He will continue to oversee our world and to remain faithful to all His covenant promises. Satan may well fuel the evil in our world, but God has not abdicated His throne. God delights to use weak things, the whimper of Moses, the teenage Mary, the wife of a priest – all to further His purposes and frustrate the foe.

The Effect of One Man

The care of Joash and his return to the throne were orchestrated by the priest, Jehoiada. With a keen sense of timing, with wisdom, and with skill, Jehoiada planned the day when the king was "unveiled." The day of manifestation had arrived (2 Kings 11). His exercise was for the king to have his place in the kingdom and in the hearts of God's people. Here is the challenge facing priestly men today: to so exalt Christ in the midst of His people, that all will enthrone Him and own Him.

When the day of unveiling arrived, Jehoiada armed the captains of the guard with the swords and shields that David had placed in the house of the Lord. The weapons were now available for use at this crisis. A man will never know the effect of his investments in spiritual things to another generation. Little did David realise that those things he had "invested" in the House of the Lord would be used to secure the throne to one of his line in a future day.

At the day of his coronation, Joash was given the testimony, the Word of God to guide him (v 12). Then he was given the crown to exalt him, and finally the removal of the rival to secure him in his position. Joash's reign began with bright promise and prospects. Through the influence of Jehoiada, it actually brought in a period of revival to the nation for a period of time.

Pause for a moment and consider the value of this godly couple and their influence on the House of God and the exaltation of God's Man. His wife acted in her sphere in a godly and Scriptural manner. Jehoiada takes the lead in the public activity. Together, they managed to bring about a time of revival and blessing to the nation. For the next 100 years, Judah would know some measure of stability through the reigns of Joash, Amaziah, Azariah, and Jotham. Joash himself, reigned for 40 years. The good which he accomplished was due, in large part, to the influence of Jehoiada. "And Joash did that which was right in the sight of the Lord all the days of Jehoiada" (2 Chron 24:2). When Jehoiada died at 130, he was buried among the kings, "because he had done much good in Israel, both toward God and toward His house" (2 Chron 24:16). The honour of being amongst the kings was a singular honour accorded to this priest who had been such a blessing to the nation.

An end that was Ignoble

Joash is a man who began well when he had positive influences in his life; but he ended very poorly due to the evil influence of the princes (2 Chron 24). It appears that his later years reversed everything which the former years had accomplished.

The princes of Judah turned Joash from following the Lord (2 Chron 24:17, 18). The apostasy was so great that we read that "wrath came upon Judah and Jerusalem for their trespass" (v 18). God in mercy sent prophets who, sadly, were ignored. We are given the tragic story of one particular prophet. His name was Zechariah, the son of Jehoiada the priest who had been so influential in Joash's earlier days, and whose mother had saved Joash from Athaliah.

We are told that the Spirit of God "clothed" him, an indication of the sincere and urgent attempt of God to get the attention of the nation. His witness was solemn and faithful as he warned of the consequences of forsaking the Lord.

To our amazement, we are told that the people conspired against him and stoned him to death. But then it is added that it was at the command of the king. Thus, the king was responsible for the stoning of the son of the couple who had done so much for him. He stoned his cousin to death to silence the voice of God.

There is irony on top of irony as we are told that it was in the "court of the house of the Lord" (v 21) the place where Jehoiada had crowned him as king. When Joash was crowned, the priest was very careful to avoid any execution in the House of the Lord. But Joash had no such scruples. Zechariah was slain in the House which had been Joash's haven of safety for six years.

The sad comment by the inspired writer is, "Thus Joash remembered not the kindness which Jehoiada his father had done to him, but slew his son" (v 22). It is a sad reality that kindness and large-heartedness on the part of believers is not always rewarded in kind in this life. Many are those who have extended themselves for other believers, only to be hurt by them in future days. The apostle Paul experienced this from some of the churches in which he had laboured. At the end of his days, "no man stood with him." The Lord Jesus is the ultimate example of doing good and receiving evil in return.

We are told that when Zechariah died, he said, "The Lord look upon it and require it." This was likely more a cry for justice than for vengeance.

But the curtain has not fallen finally on the story of this pious couple and their son. It is left for the Lord Jesus to write the concluding chapter. In Matthew 23, the Lord was reviewing the recalcitrant attitude and stubborn hearts of the nation down through the years. He pierces the natural heart of man and his defiant attitude to the voice of God. He summarises the rebellion of men by bringing a charge against the nation when He said, "that upon you may come all the righteous blood shed upon the earth, from the blood of righteous Abel, unto the blood of Zacharias, the son of Barachias, whom ye slew between the temple and the altar (Matt 23:35). (There is some debate due to the name of Barachias introduced here). It must be remembered that 2 Chronicles was the last book in the Hebrew Bible. The Lord in this manner is saying the equivalent of our, "from Genesis to Revelation." The blood that Joash shed was righteous blood. The Lord honoured His servant almost a millennia later by publicly owning his righteousness.

Jonathan

"There is one friend in the life of each of us who seems not a separate person, however dear and beloved, but an expansion, an interpretation of oneself."

Reading: 1 Samuel 18:1-4; 19:1-6; 20:24-34; 23:15-18

I hope that I will be forgiven for including Jonathan in this compendium of "minor" characters. It can well be argued that he is not really a minor person on the landscape of Scripture. He is mentioned in many chapters in 1 Samuel and several of his exploits are detailed. But I have heard him maligned so often, I would like to vindicate him in some measure. He was not perfect (and maybe neither are we). He is criticised for not being with David in the cave; for staying with his father, Saul. Attention is drawn to the fact that he died in battle side by side with Saul, rather than standing with David. He is defamed because he did not go to the cave but chose the city. All this despite feeling the hurled javelin from his father because of his devotion to David; despite his speaking for David and the encouragement he provided.

In Jonathan, the Spirit of God paints one of the loveliest portraits of devotion and fidelity that we have in Scripture. In him we will see the marks of true devotion and discipleship. He scores very high on the scale that measures friendship. Despite the malicious intentions of men and women with an agenda, there was nothing illicit or immoral in the affection between Jonathan and David.

The Measure of a Man

Consider first the kind of man of whom we are speaking. The measure of the man can be taken by looking not only at what he accomplished but why, how, and under what circumstances. Though Saul stood head and shoulders above the rest of the nation physically, Jonathan stands head and shoulders above his father morally, in his courage and in his confidence in the Lord.

In 1 Samuel 13, Jonathan takes the initiative in confronting he Philistine enemy. With a smaller company than followed Saul, he was able to smite the garrison of the Philistines and gain the victory. Yet, Saul is given the credit (v 4), and Jonathan raises no voice in opposition. Again, as the enemy reacted and rose up to fight, it is Jonathan who takes the battle to the foe (ch 14), His courage and confidence in God are remarkable. While Saul is trembling with the host, Jonathan is trusting with his armor bearer, ascending to face the enemy. How often have the words of Jonathan been an encouragement to believers: "There is no restraint of God to save by many or by few" (1 Sam 14:6). Once again victory is obtained. The only thing which marred the day of victory was Saul's rash curse which would have brought death to Jonathan had the people not intervened.

An entire sermon could be added here about his eyes being "enlightened" by the honey, and linking the honey with the Word of God (Ex 16:31; Ps 19:10; 119:103). Allow this to be an additional meditation you develop on your own.

Jonathan was marked, as well, by a motive far different from his father. Saul wanted to be avenged of his enemies (ch 14:24), while Jonathan saw them as the "uncircumcised Philistines" whom the Lord could defeat (14:5-7). Jonathan rose above his father. It is encouraging to realise that our children can outstrip us in their exploits for God. And it should be our prayer that our children do indeed rise higher than we have risen, accomplishing greater feats for the Lord. It is encouraging to realise that one generation may exceed the previous generation. The spiral does not have to be downward!

Later, when Jonathan made a covenant with David, his concern was for the next generation. He wanted his family to be preserved and useful. He excelled over the previous generation and, doubtless, he wanted the next generation to rise above him.

The Making of a Disciple

The battle had been fought and David had conquered the feared giant, Goliath. He ascended the valley and presented the trophy of his victory to Saul. Jonathan, Saul's son was there observing the youth who had descended into the shadow of death to save him and the army. As Saul's oldest son, he was in line for the throne. What he does is the most unnatural thing. No one had more reason to be jealous of David than Jonathan. Yet he strips himself of his garments, sword, and bow, laying everything at David's feet.

Jonathan was likely older than David since he had a family by this point in time. Notice the triumph of love: it is an older man giving place to a younger man as more fit; the royal son giving way to a shepherd boy, and the claimant to the throne to a potential rival. Everything was contrary to the natural order.

Here was a heart that was captivated by David, a saviour. In placing his sword and bow, the tokens of his strength and talent at David's feet, we see hands that were consecrated to David from that day forward. It is interesting and perhaps significant that when we read the tragic end of Saul and Jonathan in 1 Samuel 31, the enemy stripped Saul, but it does not mention that they stripped Jonathan. He had already stripped himself of his garments and placed them at the feet of David.

More significantly, in all his actions, Jonathan was placing David on the throne of his heart and all his hopes for the future were channelled to David. Henceforth, he was owning David as his lord.

The practical aspect of all of this upon us as believers is obvious. Have we placed all at the feet of the one Who is greater than David? Does He have the throne of my heart? Has all my life been turned over to Him to use as He sees best? Natural ability, while not a spiritual gift, can be yielded to Him for His use, as well as my time.

It was the sight of a man who offered himself and faced death for him that captivated his heart. The victor in the valley had won Jonathan's heart. We read that his soul was knit to David. We are not only linked with Christ, but we are in Christ. He appreciated not only David's skill, but his character.

The Marks of Devotion

Jonathan displayed all the true marks of devotion to David. Notice the:

The Sacrifices He Made

He gave place to David and recognised that the throne would be his. When he removed his royal robe and laid it at David's feet, he was in effect owning David as the rightful heir to the throne. He was not consumed by what Shakespeare called the "Green Eyed Monster," but could value another and own his worth. The assembly at Corinth was populated and almost destroyed by a spirit of competition with each wanting to display his gift to the exclusion of the others. How different the "mind of Christ" that seeks the honour of others rather than self (Phil 2:5-8).

He Spoke up for David

It was in a hostile atmosphere, poisoned by his father's hatred, fear, jealousy, and anger (ch 19:4-6), that he spoke up on David's behalf. Then, he defended David again, this time in a more public venue (ch 20:27-34). The result was that he experienced shame for David. He interceded for David and sought to be a peacemaker. He shows respect for his father in the manner in which he speaks, but faithfully represents David.

It appears that he confronted his father initially in private, which was a wise move. He reminds Saul that David had put his life on the line for him. He is seen moving between David and his father to bring about peace. While doing so, he is sacrificing his own position as heir to the throne. He deserves the title of the "Peacemaker who is Blessed indeed" for his efforts to reconcile his father to David.

The Suffering He Endured

As a result of faithfulness to David, the javelin meant for David was aimed at him (ch 20). He endured reproach heaped on him by his father for his devotion to David. As a result of being identified with David, he received the treatment intended for David. The hatred of the natural heart of Saul for David found a visible object in Jonathan.

We are reminded in all of this of how the natural heart responded to Christ and to those who represent Him in this scene. When He was here, the Lord Jesus endured the reproach which the hearts of men would have heaped upon God were He visible and available to them. "The reproaches of them that reproached Thee are fallen upon me" (Ps 69:9). Those who, in turn, represent Christ in our society, will endure reproach in some form, for Him.

He Shielded David

Jonathan went to great lengths to shield David from danger and discovery by Saul. His great concern was David's honour and eventual exaltation to the throne. The defending of his name in the court (ch 19), and the elaborate schemes for transmitting information (ch 20), were all an indication of how carefully and zealously he proved his love for David.

Do I shield the name and honour of Christ from reproach and dishonour? Is this a priority in my life? Our lives testify either to His worth or they bring dishonour upon Him.

The Ministry of Encouragement

One of the most touching scenes in the story of Jonathan is recounted in 1 Samuel 23. Saul, hunting for David, was not able to find him. Yet, Jonathan could find out the place where David was hiding. We read that he came to David "in the wood" and strengthened his hand in God. Jonathan was able to supply the greatly valued ministry of encouragement. He ministered this encouragement by reminding him of the Word of God and its promises. "Thou shalt be king over Israel."

Many believers know what it is to be "in the woods" of discouragement and uncertainty. The believer who is able to come alongside and encourage is an invaluable asset to any assembly. This is true friendship. Notice, however, what gave David encouragement. It was a reminder of the Word of God. This is our source of help one to another. Think of others who served as encouragements in times of distress. Onesiphorus brought encouragement to Paul in the dungeon in Rome; Naomi to Ruth in Bethlehem; and Ittai by his confession to David in his flight from Absalom.

Seek to be an encouragement to some believer today.

The Memorial to a Friend

David's knowledge of the death of Saul and Jonathan evoked the elegy which has become known as the "Song of the Bow." David's appreciation for Jonathan is both touching and tragic. Here was a friend whose love excelled the natural love that marks women, with their seeming boundless love for family. "Very pleasant hast thou been unto me" (2 Sam 1:26), summarised the life of this faithful friend. Here was a friend of whom Solomon could write, "the sweetness of a man's friend (rejoices) by hearty counsel" (Pro 27:9), and "Iron sharpeneth iron, so a man sharpeneth the countenance of his friend" (27:17).

David did not exaggerate in honouring his friend Jonathan. He paid tribute to the value and preciousness of a true friend.

David's affection for Jonathan is seen in one final scene. In 2 Samuel 9, David proved faithful to his covenant promise to Jonathan. He brought Mephibosheth from a distant land to sit at his table as one of the king's sons. Jonathan never occupied that place, but his son was able to enjoy the presence of David. His presence at the table was a constant reminder of how much David valued Jonathan.

Joseph of Arimathaea

"The mark of a great man is one who knows when to set aside the important things in order to accomplish the vital ones."

Reading: *Matthew 27:57-60; Mark 15:42-46; Luke 23:50-54; John 19:38-42*

Insight From the Gospels

Joseph of Arimathaea stepped out of the shadows of obscurity and provided one of the most remarkable services for the Lord ever recorded. He exemplifies a man who seizes the moment and rises to heights of usefulness, an example for all who follow.

Each gospel account is unique, each stressing a different aspect of the man and his ministry. In Matthew, he is a rich man and supplicant. In Mark he is a reliable servant and separated, in Luke he is a righteous man who is waiting, and in John he is a ready man who is discreet.

There are only a few brief verses in each of the gospel records that give us insight into the life and person of Joseph of Arimathaea. Here is a man who rose to meet a crisis and, as a result, will be honoured eternally. The four gospel records highlight differing aspects of his person and his actions.

Matthew stresses for us that he was a rich man. Matthew, of course, wants us to hear the words of Isaiah 53 that "He was with the rich in His death." God brought a rich man to honour His Son in His burial.

It is often pointed out that we have a rich man "begging" (v 58), the word employed, "*aiteo,*" can also mean to ask or desire. It may be a bit too much to read the thought of begging into it.

Matthew also stresses that it was his "own new tomb." Here was a man who was willing to make a huge sacrifice to honour his Lord.

A tomb in Jerusalem would be a valuable asset. To be buried in the ancient and holy city would be a great honour. Matthew also tells us that the body of the Lord Jesus was wrapped in "fine" linen. The first mention of fine linen is in connection with another Joseph (Gen 41:42). It was part of Joseph's vindication as he stood before Pharaoh, in effect, owning his righteousness. Likewise, the fine linen purchased and used by Joseph of Arimathaea was a sign of the value he placed on the Lord Jesus and of His righteous character.

Mark adds another touch to the profile when he tells us about the character of Joseph, that he was an honourable counsellor. Here was a man who did his job well. The Perfect Servant is going to be buried by a servant of the people who was honourable in his work. Along with his character, his courage is highlighted as we are told that he went in boldly to Pilate and craved (once again our word, "aiteo") the body of Jesus. Many commentators suggest that in the original language, there is a contrast in the word "body" in verses 43 and 45. The former is body while Pilate in verse 45 refers to it as a corpse.

Another feature about Joseph which Mark adds is that he was waiting for the kingdom of heaven. He was one of a small remnant who believed God and looked forward to a coming King and kingdom.

Luke's comments are worthy of note. The charges against the Lord Jesus in Luke's account are very personal. He was labeled a "Perverter of the people" (Luke 23:2). It is as though heaven cannot allow this slur to pass unchallenged. Thus, at the cross, the centurion confesses "certainly this was a righteous man" (v 47), and Joseph is characterised as a "good man and just" (v 50). God brings a good man to bury a "good Man." His separation from the evil of the Sanhedrin is also stressed by recounting that he had not consented to their counsel. He stood aloof from the injustice. But he was not standing idle. He moved and came forward to request the body of the Lord Jesus.

Another vital detail that Luke tells us of is that the tomb which Joseph provided was one in which never before had a body been placed. Keep this seemingly minor detail in mind when we come to the importance of what Joseph did.

Finally *John* adds vital information not provided by other writers. We have all heard sermons about Joseph being a secret disciple who took courage after the cross and went to Pilate. Bear in mind that the original manuscripts did not have punctuation. As a result, the placing of commas was an area in which translators had liberty according to their understanding of the sentence. It very likely means, not that he was a secret disciple, but that he went secretly to Pilate fearing that if the Jews knew he was going to give the body of the Lord Jesus an honourable burial, they would have objected. Others details unique to John's account include the addition of Nicodemus, the myrrh and aloes amounting to almost 100 pounds in weight, and that rather than any changes to the body as might have occurred in either a Roman or Egyptian burial, the type of burial was a Jewish one in which no changes were made to the body.

Nicodemus brought 100 pounds of myrrh and aloes. A burial of a King. Give what you have for Him. Mary gave a pound of spikenard ointment, it was all she had. Nicodemus gave 100 pounds; she gave in the house and was criticised; he gave openly and was ostracised.

John also tells us that He was buried in a garden. In fact, it is only John who tells us that Gethsemane was also a garden. Thus the work of salvation was accomplished between two gardens, perhaps a contrast with the first garden being intended. Life, a major theme in John, was lost in a garden. Eternal life was procured between two gardens.

Matthew has stressed his capability as a rich man; Mark his courage; Luke his character; John his care.

Foresight

Did Joseph have foresight about the cross and the need for a burial place for his Saviour? Had he prepared the tomb for the Lord Jesus or did he move spontaneously as he saw the need? Definitive answers are difficult to give, but in light of the very few who grasped the coming events, it is safe to assume that he was motivated by devotion and love. He did not sense the coming events and the need there might be for a tomb.

But foresight was at work on that memorable day. Assuming that the dismissal of His spirit by the Lord occurred somewhere in the area of 3.00pm, and that the Jewish Sabbath commenced at 6.00pm, Joseph had a mere three hours to accomplish all he did. He had three hours in which to accomplish the very work for which he had been born. To be born again is a great blessing. To know for what work you have been born again is an even greater blessing.

In a very real sense when Joseph and Nicodemus buried the body of the Lord Jesus, they were burying their future with the Jewish nation. No longer would they be members of the Sanhedrin. No longer would they be respected as part of the Jewish community. They were dead and buried as far as their society was concerned. What is symbolised at our baptism, took place for these two men when they undertook the work of burial.

Hindsight

Looking back, consider all that was accomplished by this act of devotion, even apart from an honourable burial being given to the Lord.

As noted, it accomplished Scripture and fulfilled prophecy.

It was a testimony to Pilate that the Lord was dead. He inquired of the centurion since he knew that death was a slow process and marveled to hear that the Lord was already dead. This negates all the theorists who claim the Lord swooned on the cross and then revived in the coolness of Joseph's tomb. A centurion who had witnessed countless deaths attested to the death of the Lord Jesus.

But perhaps the greatest value in this careful record of the honourable burial lies is the apologetic for the veracity of a resurrection. The bodies of "criminals" who were crucified were left for vultures. Just remember those crucified at the Spartacus rebellion.

The Jews, in turn, if allowed, would bury them outside the city in a place where those executed were placed in a common grave, or worse still, burned in the valley of Hinnon. This would have made proof for the Lord's resurrection impossible.

Also, here is a new tomb, only one way in and one way out. A great stone is placed at its entrance and soldiers are stationed to guard it. An empty tomb needs an explanation. Claiming disciples came by night to steal him away is ludicrous in light of the guard.

"After the manner of the Jews" assures us that there was no embalming or mutilation of the body. It was the same body which came out of the tomb which had gone into the tomb.

Another small detail is that no other body had ever been laid to rest in that tomb. Recall the story back in 2 Kings 13. As a man was being buried, an emergency made it necessary to throw his body into a tomb which happened to be that of Elisha. When the dead man's body touched the bones of Elisha, he was revived. The virtue for his resurrection lay in the bones of Elisha, not in the man. Had a body been in Joseph's tomb, the Jews could have argued that what happened in 2 Kings 13 had happened here again.

The basis for resurrection was established by the care with which Joseph buried the Lord Jesus.

One additional thought. Recall that in John 18, the Jews did not wish to defile themselves by entering into the judgment hall. Ironically, they wanted to be able to eat Passover, despite the fact that they were crucifying the ultimate Passover.

In handling the dead body of the Lord Jesus Christ, Joseph and Nicodemus had no fear or concern about defilement. Was it because they recognised that this body could not defile them? That He was holy even in death? Or was it because they realised they no longer needed a Passover symbol since they now had the reality? We are not told. Perhaps it was both. But their readiness to handle that precious body was testimony to all of the uniqueness of the person whose body they were handling.

Joseph of Arimathaea was a man who makes a very brief appearance on the stage of history but whose act has an eternal consequence.

Joseph the Carpenter

"Say little, serve all, pass on."

James Boyd

Reading: *Matthew 1:18-25; 2:13-23*

The gospel of Luke centres primarily on Mary in the narrative of the announcement, incarnation, and birth of the Lord Jesus. Matthew, in turn, throws the spotlight on Joseph. It is in a dream that Joseph is told of Mary and exhorted to marry her. It is in dreams that Joseph is warned of Herod and his plot to kill the child. Joseph is seen moving in obedience to God throughout chapters 1 and 2. Then, he fades from the story. Though only a few chapters tell us about him, his is nevertheless, a life worthy of note. Consider the following:

Lowliness of His Occupation

The fortunes of the House of David had fallen on troubled times. The heir to the throne is not in Jerusalem but in a Galilean village of ill-repute, Nazareth. He is not wielding the sceptre of power but the instruments of a carpenter. Rather than making decisions of state he is making furniture and other implements for household use.

The sceptics, if there were any at the time in Judea, could well have called into question God's promises to David. What had happened to the promise of an everlasting dynasty (2 Sam 7:16)? His throne was to be established forever, yet Israel was now ruled by an Edomite who sat on the throne and over him was a Roman king sitting on his throne in Rome.

Though there is a more critical reason, the wisdom of God can be seen, however, in His selection of Joseph as the legal father of the Lord

Jesus. In light of the movement to Egypt, time spent there, journey back to Israel, and turning aside to Nazareth, a man whose occupation was carpentry would be able to find work wherever he travelled. Some occupations would be location specific. But carpentry is one which is always in demand, regardless of location.

One of the trials of life for every believer is the reconciling of divine promises and purposes with circumstances that arise in life. Who has not struggled at one time or another with the negative circumstances of life over against the promises of God? The two who trod the road to Emmaus knew firsthand the dilemma of the "facts" they faced and the prospects that Scripture had promised. They, as we, had the problem of one-sided theology. They needed their thinking and reasoning balanced which is what the Lord did when He opened to their understanding "all" the Scriptures.

The Sensitivity of His Outlook

We are told that Joseph was a just man, yet he was also marked by a tenderness and care for Mary. Doubtless he struggled with the events which were transpiring before him. How could the pious girl to whom he was betrothed be with child? He knew he was not responsible. She had spent the last three months in the home of a godly couple, Zacharias and Elisabeth, away from evil influences.

In his love for Mary, he decided not to make her a public example, but intended to handle the "putting away' in a quiet and private manner. His care for her is touching and exemplary. He reminds us that we can combine grace and truth in all our actions, even those that are disciplinary in nature.

His willingness to obey the Scriptures is suddenly balanced by the message from the angel concerning the source of Mary's conception. All is now resolved by the Word of God.

Readiness of His Obedience

Joseph is marked by action rather than eloquence. In fact, we never hear he speak a word throughout the verses that tell us about him.

It is his ready obedience that commands our attention. Throughout Matthew 1 and 2, whenever he is given a revelation or command from the Lord via the angel, he carries it out without delay. He is told to take Mary to be his wife which he does (1:20). He is instructed to flee into Egypt (2:14) and he obeys. He is told to return to the land of Israel (2:21) and then, when warned by God concerning Archelaus, he turns aside to Nazareth.

He is never seen negotiating with God, compromising, or delaying, but always obeying immediately. Like the Psalmist, he will run in the way of God's commandments (Ps 119:32).

Does obedience mark my life in regard to the Word of God? Many of us have become so adept of rationalising or spiritualising truth, that we justify our delay. How vital to remember that partial or delayed obedience is really disobedience. Saul learned to his loss that God delights in obedience and the surrender of our wills. In Eden, Adam exalted his will above God's. The Last Adam, yielded His will in perfect obedience to God. All those who are linked with this last Adam should be marked by a surrender of will to the Lord. "Hath the LORD as great delight in burnt offerings and sacrifices, as in obeying the voice of the LORD? Behold, to obey is better than sacrifice, and to hearken than the fat of rams" (1 Sam 15:22).

Assuming of an Obligation

There are two statements which indicate that Joseph willingly assumed a responsibility that the Angel of the Lord had required of him: "He took unto him his wife," and then, "He called His name, Jesus." In taking Mary and then in naming the child, he became the stepfather, the legal father of the Child Who was to be born. There, once again, is no hint of reluctance or hesitation. He moves in obedience to the command of God.

Here is a man who has the Word of God for his partner in life. "Take unto thee Mary thy wife." God may not speak as directly and clearly as He did to Joseph, yet it is still important that a couple contemplating marriage have something from the Word of God to encourage them in the step they are taking. Joseph could for the rest of his marriage look back with the assurance that their marriage was according to the will of God.

Joseph named the child in keeping with the direction given him (1:21). Though we never hear Joseph speak, we do know one word which he uttered. He named the child "Jesus." Here is the one word to which we are privy, that came from the lips of this godly man. If one word has to summarise the speech of one's life, this is certainly the best!

Acceptance of an Onus

When Joseph married Mary, and when he also named the child, he was taking responsibility for them both. He was, in the eyes of his society, taking responsibility for the child. All would assume that Joseph was the father. Just as Mary bowed to the will of God, yielding her body and her future to the Lord, so Joseph was accepting life-long reproach in his naming of the child.

Avoidance of an Obstacle

Joseph's genealogy is traced back through Coniah or Jeconiah. This presents a problem in light of the prophecy by Jeremiah in Jeremiah 22:30, "Thus saith the LORD, Write ye this man childless, a man that shall not prosper in his days: for no man of his seed shall prosper, sitting upon the throne of David, and ruling any more in Judah." Thus, no one of the seed of Jeconiah would have the legal right to sit on the throne of David. That would have been one obstacle to overcome. But then, since Mary was not through Solomon, that presents another barrier. But Christ was not the seed of Jeconiah. If we consider Mary's genealogy as given in Luke 3, we find that she came through Nathan and not his brother Solomon. He is therefore not of the seed of Jeconiah.

Having been born to Mary, the Lord Jesus is the seed of the woman and also the seed of David. But since royalty ended with Jeconiah,

His right to the throne is guaranteed by His adoption by Joseph, thus making Joseph His legal father, although not His literal father. God in His infinite wisdom brought together two different lines from David, one from Solomon through Jeconiah, and the other through Nathan, avoiding the curse on Jeconiah and his seed. As John Riddle insightfully points out in WTBT, "If Christ came through him (Coniah), He would not be able to sit upon the throne. In Luke we evidently have the line of Mary the daughter of Heli, Joseph's father-in-law, through Nathan, thus preserving the bloodline of David while avoiding the curse of Coniah."

Mephibosheth

"And be ye kind one to another, tenderhearted, forgiving one another, even as God for Christ's sake hath forgiven you"

Ephesians 4:32

Reading: *2 Samuel 4:4; 9:6-13; 16:1-4; 19:24-30*

It is difficult, if not impossible, to avoid rushing into the gospel mode whenever we hear the story of Mephibosheth. The application to our condition as sinners is so patent that any other approach seems contrived and misapplied. His descent from the family of an enemy, his disability at the age of five from a fall, his distance in a far country, the deliverance by grace, and the distinction of sitting at the king's table – these and other details all remind us of our own condition and how grace has so bountifully blessed us, and, as a result, they all plead for a gospel application.

I have no illusions that from henceforth and forevermore gospel application will not be the primary manner in which this story will be handled. But will you allow me the liberty of looking at some other lessons which can be learned from his life? Some details of that life are spread over several chapters in 2 Samuel including chapters 4, 9, 19, and 21. Though he makes more than a cameo appearance, he is still a minor character worthy of note.

The Tragedy That Befell Him

Here is a man who should have been a prince, yet due to the negligence of a nurse early in his life, he is in a far-off place. A tragic accident due to her failure in his care resulted in ruined prospects.

Unaware of the bond between Mephibosheth's father and David, the nurse thought that the only recourse was a hasty retreat.

Paul spoke of his care for the Thessalonian believers and likened it to that of a nursing mother who cherished her children (1 Thess 2:7). (He also likened his care to that of a father in v 11). Overseers must assume many roles. On the one hand they are shepherds who feed the flock. They are guides who show the way. They are leaders who lead by example. But if the imagery of the Perfect Shepherd of Isaiah 40 is our prototype, there is a nurturing and nursing aspect to leadership, especially with young believers, that is formative in their Christian experience.

The story of Mephibosheth reminds us of how important the early years of development can be. What occurred at the age of five left its mark on him for the remainder of his life. Grace overcame but did not erase the evidence of the tragedy. There is no question about the wisdom demanded in caring for new converts and young believers. The encouragement that many need must be balanced by the restraint that a few may require. The personal interest shown to each is helpful as they begin to experience some of the problems of the Christian life. The leaders mentioned in Hebrews 13:7 were men worthy of emulation, having guided the flock by the Word of God. The story of Mephibosheth should be a clarion call to all who shepherd the young that care is vital for the eventual growth and usefulness of young believers. Future growth may be hindered by unwise handling (or manhandling) in early years. Had the nurse remembered that there was a covenant of grace which embraced Mephibosheth, she would have acted differently. We who lead and shepherd must always remember that each new believer is an object of divine grace, precious to the Shepherd, and needing our wise care.

The Recovery He knew

The failure of a nurse is now matched by the skill of a man who sought his recovery. David the king sought him out and brought him from a place of distance to be as one of the king's sons. The recovery of someone who is at a distance, no longer spiritually useful, and away from the assembly, is a skill that is very rare. Straying believers, like sheep, do not seek out shepherds. The shepherd must go after the sheep. The Lord Jesus taught a vital lesson in two of His parables when He justified His healing ministry on the Sabbath. In Luke 14 He used the parable of the ox or ass having fallen into a ditch. In this instance, the beast had to be pulled out of the ditch (Luke 14:5). But in Matthew 12 He related a similar parable but this time the victim in the ditch was a sheep. In this instance, the sheep had to be "lifted" out. Greater care and a more personal involvement is seen in lifting versus pulling. Some try to pull young believers out by the neck, but it leads to strangulation. Sheep need a person to come near, feel the burden, and lift them from the traps into which they have fallen.

The Dignity Conferred

David is able to bring Mephibosheth from a far country where he lingered, to sit at the king's table as one of his sons. Though Mephibosheth is very conscious of the grace which has been showered upon him, David does nothing to make him feel anything less than welcome and at home. David makes it abundantly clear that he stands in all the acceptability of his father, Jonathan. The oath made between David and Jonathan assures a steady stream of grace flowing to Mephibosheth.

Restoration involves not only a person being brought back to assembly fellowship, but "sitting at the king's table" once again and enjoying the benefits of sonship. Perhaps it is the emphasis on grace and the appreciation of grace that makes this possible.

Joseph is a prime example of a man who was able to restore his brethren. He never once mentioned their sin to them prior to their repentance. And then he only mentioned it to reassure them that he has seen the hand of God in every detail of the ordeal. Even though as late as Genesis 50, the consciences of the brothers still haunt them, Joseph is able to place all the events in a context which enables his forgiveness to be received as he spoke kindly to them (v 21).

All those who nurse and nurture younger men and women should seek to inculcate into them the awareness of their acceptability before God and the fact that God, if there has been failure, is a God of recovery. Where there has not been failure, the encouragement and nurturing of young lives is the best way to ensure growth and usefulness in the future.

The Defamation He Experienced

At the time of David's hasty escape from Jerusalem, Ziba, seeing his opportunity to ingratiate himself with David, falsely accused Mephibosheth of the very sin of which he, himself, was guilty – opportunism. Mephibosheth's lameness prohibited him from following David without the aid of Ziba. The result was that appearances were deceiving and Ziba went alone to meet David. He defames his master, hoping that David will give him all that once belonged to Mephibosheth. In an uncharacteristic style, David acted hastily and conferred all that belonged to Mephibosheth on Ziba. The ploy was successful and Ziba appeared to have triumphed, and Mephibosheth appeared to have lost.

The Behaviour He Manifested

How do we react when falsely accused, when misrepresented? For Mephibosheth, the options were limited. He could not chase after David and plead his case. He was isolated in Jerusalem with a usurper claiming the throne; possibly his own life was in jeopardy.

It was nothing short of divine wisdom which guided him in his actions. How could he show loyalty to the absent king? What could he do to possibly prove to David, if he were able to return, that he had not been unfaithful?

We read, "Mephibosheth the son of Saul came down to meet the king, and had neither dressed his feet, nor trimmed his beard, nor washed his clothes, from the day the king departed until the day he came again in peace" (19:24). The tokens of mourning for his absent benefactor were obvious for David to see. Rather than a celebratory mood with hopes of a regained kingdom, Mephibosheth had been marked by mourning. He so lived, that all men knew where his allegiance lay. He had been faithful to David in his absence.

Are we marked by faithfulness? That does not mean we should not shave, wash our clothes, or clean ourselves, but it does suggest that we should be marked by a sense of longing for the return of the King.

The Choice He Made

The blessing or the blesser? The gift or the giver? Abraham faced this choice when called to sacrifice the blessing, Isaac, to obey the word of the One Who gave him the blessing. The Saviour faced this as the ultimate temptation in Matthew's account. Would He accept the blessing of the kingdoms of this world or would He, in faithfulness to His God, only accept them by way of the cross? While failure and sin were impossible for Him, it is still noteworthy that His response to Satan was, if I may be allowed to paraphrase, "I will worship and serve God even if it means a cross!"

Mephibosheth came to meet David on his return from self-imposed exile (2 Sam 19:24). Did David recognise at once the faithfulness of Mephibosheth? Was he testing him by his questions? Undoubtedly, the appearance of Mephibosheth who had not shaved or changed his clothes since the day David fled from the city, must have made some impression on David.

"Thou and Ziba divide the land," were David's words to his adopted son. The test is applied. How does Mephibosheth respond? "Let him take all forasmuch as my lord the king is come again in peace unto his own house" (v 30). Mephibosheth displayed his loyalty and love for David by his words. (Incidentally, is this where Solomon learned a lesson which he applied in judging the two harlots?)

Mephibosheth, in his expression of contentment with David's return, displayed that he cared more about the person than any possessions, more for the source of grace than the gifts he had received.

Lessons

- The crucial role of nursing young believers
- The skill needed to help recovery when there has been a fall
- The tokens of loyalty that we can display
- The choice we may face between the gift and the Giver
- And yes, keep preaching the gospel from the story of Mephibosheth

Nathan

"Crisis does not create character. It reveals it."

Reading: *2 Samuel 7:1-17; 1 Kings 1:11-37*

There were three men, all prophets, who were notably influential in David's life: Samuel for his preparation and molding, Gad (1 Sam 22; 2 Sam 24) the Seer who was with him in his rejection, and Nathan the Prophet who was with him in several crisis situations.

Nathan was present at three pivotal points in David's career that also touch, either directly or typically, on the person of Christ. Nathan had to grow in each of his encounters. He had to face progressive opposition in each confrontation: himself, the king, and the nation behind Adonijah.

While profit can be derived from considering all three of these prophets, we will concern ourselves for the present with Nathan the prophet and extract from his life some lessons for our spiritual help. The significance of these events can be seen in that he rises to the challenge and is responsible on the human level for the will of God concerning David to be fulfilled. There is always the balance between divine sovereignty and human responsibility.

Nathan and the House of God

After many years, and after many obstacles, David finally enjoyed peace in his realm. He had not only unified the nation, but had subdued many of Israel's long-time foes. He had defeated the Philistines and brought the ark up to Jerusalem. He sat as king, undisputed and unrivaled. He was, however, very conscious of the goodness of God that had brought him to this place and, as he thought upon it, felt a desire to build God a house.

A consciousness of grace should always motivate us to desire to build up each other, and to build up God's assembly. Grace is the great motivator in the Christian life.

This desire was confided by David to Nathan the prophet. It seemed incongruous that he, David, should dwell in a fine stately home and the ark of God be consigned to a tent within curtains. Nathan, recognising the nobility of David's desire and this inconsistency as well, gave David his approval for his exercise.

What may seem like the obvious thing to do, may not always be the will of God. God's will must be carried out in God's time by God's man. This was not the time, nor was David the man. So, that very night, God spoke to Nathan in a vision and corrected his thinking, giving him instructions to go again to David and deliver God's message to him. We read of Nathan that, "according to all these words, and according to all this vision, so did Nathan speak unto David" (2 Sam 7:17). He was careful with every word that God gave him to utter.

There would be some embarrassment perhaps on the part of the prophet. He had to admit to himself that he had been hasty in giving his approval. For a man in a place of prominence such as Nathan would have been, to admit error, is not an easy mater. To his credit, he is quick to obey the Lord and own his mistaken advice to David. The message that he delivered to David was of a different nature but of eternal significance. How important that message was can only be appreciated in light of the N. T.

Nathan shows his deep concern for the building of the House of God in God's time and under God's man. Nothing is left for human wisdom or arrangement.

God has jealously guarded construction of the Houses in which He would dwell. Moses and Solomon were both men of wisdom. Moses was learned in all that Egypt could provide of engineering instruction. They had built the great pyramids whose construction still amazes modern engineers. Solomon was the wisest man in the earth. Yet God did not leave them to fill in details for either the tabernacle or temple. All was made "according to the pattern."

In the N. T. Paul is the faithful man similar to Nathan who knows God's pattern. Paul was very concerned that the believers in Corinth were not building according to the pattern.

He makes abundantly clear that the existence of the problems in the assembly were inconsistent with the pattern God had for a local company. In:

1 Cor 1-4   Divisions - Inconsistency in relation to the person of Christ

Ch 5   Defilement - Immorality in light of the Passover

Ch 6   Disputation - Improbity in light of the Kingdom

Ch 7-9   Devotion - Indispensability in light of the Priority

Ch 10-14   Disorder - Incompatibility with the Spirit's Work

Ch 15   Doctrine - Implications in light of Resurrection

A Man Careful for the Holiness of God's Name

We are all familiar with the sad and tragic circumstances surrounding David's moral collapse. For perhaps a year, God was silent. Psalm 51 suggests that David's conscience was burdened, and he knew distress of soul.

Finally, God moved in government. Once again it is Nathan who must address the crisis. He came with his parable and its unexpected sequel. David must confront his own sin and the judgment that he passed on the rich man. Nathan was instrumental in bringing about the restoration of the king. David must still face the government of God, but it will be mingled with grace.

Nathan, in facing the king, faced a greater test — that of courage to confront the man who could have taken his life if he so desired.

Other kings had shut up prophets in prison, taken their lives, or had then muzzled in some way. Jeremiah knew the experience as did the Baptist. Nathan must speak to a great man about a great sin.

He is concerned that testimony for God would suffer (v 14). He is concerned for David's restoration, but more so for God's honour and testimony among the nations. In both Jeremiah and Ezekiel (Jer 5:1; Eze 22:30), God bemoaned the fact that He sought for a man to stand in the gap for Him, someone who was concerned for the honour of His Name. He found no one. Here, in Nathan, He found a man!

Peter is the N. T. man maintaining holiness: 1 Peter 1 contains a four-fold incentive to holy living. In chapter 2 we are a holy nation and priesthood. In chapter 3 we are introduced to holy women: and in chapter 4 holy living.

2 Peter has a three-fold view of the world: dark, defiled, and doomed. In chapter 1 we are told of the Holy Mount and Holy Men. In chapter 2 he mentions Holy commandments. In chapter 3 he exhorts to Holy conversation. Holiness among the people of God is vital because, "Be ye holy for I am holy" (1 Pet 1:16).

Returning to Nathan, it takes a courageous man to speak to a great man about a great sin. Nathan rose to the challenge because the honour of God's Name was more important than the favour of the king.

But Nathan shows his balance when, having communicated the government of God, he next communicates something of the grace of God. When a little later, Bathsheba bears Solomon, it is Nathan who is sent by the Lord to give him the name Jedidiah, beloved of Jehovah (2 Sam 12:25).

A Man Concerned for the Honour of God

Failure That Occurred

The final crisis which he faced unfolded in 1 Kings 1. David was old, cold, and needed to be told what was happening in his realm. David's weaknesses with his family led to vacancy in leadership.

Adonijah quickly took advantage of this. Leadership must never have a "vacancy" sign attached to it. As with vacuums, something or someone quickly rises to fill it, and it may not be the most qualified. Adonijah thought himself, due to seniority in age, to be entitled to the throne, disregarding God's instructions concerning Solomon. The kingdom was in crisis. The purposes of God were being challenged. Once again, Nathan enters the scene.

Fellowship He Kept

Nathan is seen moving in consort with the priest, Zadok, and with Benaiah. He will not walk in the counsel of the ungodly nor stand in the way of sinners. He is separated from all the evil and intrigue of the palace and thus, can be useful for God.

He conceives a plan with Bathsheba which is intended to have the maximal effect on David. They have one brief window of opportunity to halt the rebellion and secure the throne for Solomon as God intended. She informs David of the situation in the kingdom. Her report is corroborated by Nathan. Their combined testimony stirs David to action to secure the throne for Solomon.

Fearlessness That Marked Him

Nathan literally put his life on the line that God's testimony might endure. The Word of God concerning the future king was enough for him to move. He was concerned that the right man be on the throne. Had his efforts failed, he no doubt would have been dispatched by Adonijah as a traitor.

John is the N. T. Nathan. John enthrones Christ in the assembly of His people (John 12), in the hearts of the individual believer (1 John 5) and on the throne of the universe (Revelation 5). John's life was on the line for the sake of the Word of God and the Testimony of Jesus (Rev 1 :9). He shares with Nathan the distinction of being concerned with the rightful Man upon the throne.

Summary

His interests:

- The Temple, the Testimony, the Throne
- God's House, Holiness, Honour

His increase:

Steps to usefulness seen in Nathan's experience

- Must acknowledge his own error
- Must rebuke a king's error
- Must stand against and rebuke a nation's error (2 Kings 1)

Insights into usefulness:

- A man careful with all the Word of God (7:17)
- A man compassionate in his dealings with others (12:25)
- A man circumspect in the company he keeps (1 Kings 1)

His influence:

- Useful in God's plan for building the House of God
- Useful in maintaining a standard of righteousness
- Enthroned God's anointed in the hearts of the people and on the throne of the nation

Onesiphorus

"Encouragement is awesome. Think about it. It has the capacity to lift a man's or a woman's shoulders. To breathe fresh air into the fading embers of a smoldering dream. To actually change the course of another human being's day, week, or life."

Charles Swindoll

Reading: *2 Timothy 1:16-18*

A Breath of Fresh Air

The ministry of encouragement! How vital and how valuable it is for the people of God. Sadly, few engage in this ministry as it is not as public and visible as other forms of service. Yet, it is certainly as important to the progress of the work of God as the public gifts. In 2 Timothy 1:16-18 we read of a man, Onesiphorus, who gave himself to this ministry to the benefit of the Apostle Paul. These three verses will eternally honour him for his care and courage. Indelibly inscribed on the pages of holy writ, this testimony will follow him throughout eternal ages.

Though his biography and life work are summarised in three brief verses, they contain a wealth of insight into this faithful brother. They reveal:

His Care and Compassion

Despite the Fickleness of the Many

"Many in Asia" turned away from Paul. It was not politically safe to be identified with a criminal against the crown. Paul was too dangerous for them to link themselves with him. Despite the years of service and the tears of a faithful "father" figure, all his former friends proved fickle.

There is no suggestion here of apostasy or spiritual departure. It is likely they did not come to his legal or financial aid when he needed it. No character witnesses appeared at his trial. To be forsaken by those whom you have served is a severe trial.

Despite the Failure of Two in Particular

For some reason, two individuals are singled out as having "turned away" from the apostle: Phygellus and Hermogenes. Was their opposition singularly bitter, or were they people from whom he expected better? Just as the testimony to Onesiphorus is an eternal tribute, so the failure of these two testifies against them.

In Contrast, the Faithfulness of One

In contrast to the many and the two, there was one man who stood out. Paul says concerning him, that "he oft refreshed me." Literally, he was a breath of fresh air. This may be more literal than we can imagine if we remember Paul's imprisonment in the Mamertine prison in Rome. What an encouragement he must have been to Paul as he sought him and visited him!

His Courage and Conviction

Courage Despite

He was marked by courage despite the opinions and actions of others. We are often influence by peer pressure. This is not only a teenage problem; it continues throughout life. Onesiphorus was taking up an unpopular as well as a dangerous ministry. He could well have reasoned that his obligations as a family man limited what he could do for the apostle. The difficulties involved in merely locating Paul in the prison system were another justifiable obstacle. But Paul tells us that "he was not ashamed of my bonds." Onesiphorus had a burden and exercise and nothing was allowed to dampen it.

Convictions Held Despite

Convictions are things by which we live and things for which we are willing to die. He well knew that association with Paul was dangerous. It would have been far more convenient to "pass by on the other side" as the priest and Levite in the account of the Samaritan in Luke 10. But the convenient was not allowed to impose on the convictions which controlled his conscience and conduct.

Cost of Convictions

Convictions are costly things. Along with the investment in time, there were travel costs, expenses in supplying some of Paul's needs. There was reproach to bear, and possibly even suspicion which would arise as he linked himself with a condemned criminal.

Serving the needs of others is the standard for all believers. Those who have convictions about this ministry, soon find that it will involve cost: time, homes that are not as spotless and orderly as they might prefer, and financial expenses in entertaining and serving. Yet all is part of the treasure sent on ahead that will reap eternal dividends.

His Concern and Conscientiousness

Onesiphorus displayed diligence in finding Paul. "He sought me out very diligently" suggests that he had opportunity to turn around and go home. It was likely not easy to find him in the prison among the other prisoners. But he had made the effort earlier in Ephesus and was determined to continue now that Paul was a prisoner in Rome.

He had a spiritual desire to be of help to a believer. There are believers who would like to serve the Lord but wonder about their "gift" and ability to serve. Here is a ministry open to all.

His Consistency and Compensation

His Habits

This ministry of encouragement was not a one-time effort on the part of Onesiphorus. "He oft refreshed me ... when he was in Rome ... he ministered unto me at Ephesus" (vv16-18). This was the pattern of his life, a man who sought opportunity to be a help and cheer to others. Here was a man who made a habit of caring for others and serving them. "In prison and ye visited Me" (Matt 25:43), is the view that heaven takes of these acts of kindness.

How often do we begin with a good intention, a sincere exercise, but somewhere amidst the busyness of life and the lack of appreciation, we cease. This man was marked by consistency in his service for God.

His Honour

There was no directory for the Mamertine prison. Likely the guards would be of little help. He would have to search for Paul "very diligently" to locate his particular place of incarceration. History tells us that these "cells" were holes in the ground with no comforts or sanitation. It would involve inconvenience and time to locate someone, but that did not deter him from his exercise.

There was not only devotion involved, but determination. He would go the limit to fulfill what he felt the Lord had given him to perform.

His House

Paul's desire for Onesiphorus is that the Lord would grant mercy unto his house and that he as well would find mercy from the Lord "in that day." There is the suggestion that Onesiphorus' home and family had sacrificed to enable him to travel to minster to Paul. Paul, in turn, was looking to the Lord to preserve and bless the family. His request for Onesiphorus is open to several possible interpretations, depending on when "that day" is. Most view this as Paul's desire that the Lord would compensate him at the Bema. There can be no question that every act of kindness done in His Name now, will have its corresponding compensation then.

But another interpretation is possible. Is it possible that in identifying himself with a prisoner deemed to be an enemy of the crown, Onesiphorus was arrested and detained? "That day" could indicate a day when he would appear on trial for his "crime" against Rome. If so, Paul requests that the Lord preserve him and return him to his family.

His Heritage

Whatever outcome we posit for him, his family had a rich heritage in which they could take refuge (Prov 14:26; 20:7). He left a legacy of spiritual priority and faithful service for others, a rich legacy indeed to pass on to a future generation.

The Spirit of God has left on record the ministry of a man who was an encourager. In so doing, the Spirit's intention, likely, was not only to honour Onesiphorus, but to highlight the importance of a ministry that encourages others.

Allow your mind to roam through the pages of Scripture and think of occasions when a believer served to encourage another. We read of a Jonathan who "strengthened" David's hand in God (1 Sam 23:16). Very likely that strengthening took the form of reminding David that he would one day reign and that the promises of God would be fulfilled. It is a reminder that the vehicle of encouragement given to us is the Word of God. How important it is to have the right Word from God for the need. The Perfect Servant knew "how to speak a Word in season to him that is weary" (Isa 50:4).

And what of Ittai the Gittite? Who can measure the thrill in David's heart when Ittai proclaimed, "As the LORD liveth, and as my lord the king liveth, surely in what place my lord the king shall be, whether in death or life, even there also will thy servant be" (2 Sam 15:21). Though his own family and familiar friends turned against him, here was one lately come to Israel who remained faithful.

God the great source of all our encouragement uses humble believers to encourage His saints. While it must have been with mixed feelings of apprehension and excitement that Mary rose and travelled to the hill country to her kinsfolk, Zacharias and Elisabeth (Luke 39) I doubt she expected the welcome that she received. First, without sharing with Elisabeth the news of her conception, Elisabeth speaks of the babe in Mary's womb as "My Lord." Second, a spiritual woman such as Elisabeth, was able to accept the fact that nothing illicit had occurred and that the babe in the womb was her Lord. What a comfort and encouragement to Mary to realise that the godly in the nation would understand the virgin birth even if the majority in the nation did not.

To those already mentioned could be add the encouraging words of Moses to Joshua (Deut 1:38; 3:28), the help that Ezra was to the remnant (Ezra 8:36), In turn, Shechaniah encourages Ezra to arise and begin the work of restoration as "this matter belongs unto thee" (Ezra 10:4). Encouragers need at times to be encouraged. God in His sovereign ways and wisdom supplies that encouragement from some of the least expected sources.

We may not have the apostle Paul to visit in his Roman dungeons. But there are believers all around us who need words of encouragement. There are parents struggling with family burdens. There are mothers who are being told that they are wasting their talents in the home. There are leaders who struggle with the day-to-day problems in assembly life, and there are workers, missionaries and evangelists, who labour against all the opposition of Satan. Your word of encouragement, your note, your email, may well serve to enable them, like David, to have their hand strengthened in God, enabling them to serve more faithfully.

Rahab

"Amazing grace, how sweet the sound, that saved a wretch like me. I once was lost but now am found, was blind but now I see."

Reading: *Joshua 2:1-22*

Her Salvation

The story of Rahab is familiar to all, being used in Sunday school and in gospel meetings, times without number. We have all heard it oftened. It is significant that almost every mention of her name calls her "Rahab the harlot." Her infamous career follows her into the New Testament. But rather than being a reminder of her sinful history, it is, perhaps, to be viewed as a reminder of the grace that saved her from her wretched past.

The siege of Jericho was about to begin, and Joshua sent two spies into the city. It may be that the choice of a harlot's home for hiding was both fortuitous and wise. No doubt in light of Jericho being a stopping place for travellers, the house of the harlot would be frequented by many men, thus not drawing suspicion. Men could enter here without arousing any curiosity on the part of neighbours. Guided by the sovereign hand of God, these two spies made their way to Rahab's home.

No attempt will be made to reconcile the conflicting absolutes of truth telling and saving lives, but Rahab perhaps thought that the saving of lives was a higher good than truth telling. Her falsehoods saved the lives of the men and also ultimately brought her into spiritual blessing.

She "received the spies with peace" and after assuring the men of their safe passage, extracted from them the promise of safety in the day of Jericho's destruction. If we can trust Mr. Newberry's marginal notes, the cord hung in the window was different from the rope by which she let the men down through that window. But the cord that hung in the window was a witness to her faith and to her salvation.

God's Affirmation of Her Choice

Rahab the harlot appears in several places which at first might surprise us. As we trace the genealogies in the Old Testament, we find that Boaz was born to Salmon (one of the spies?) and Rahab (Matt 1:5). Assuming the record of Matthew 1 to be accurate, that would mean that she was the great-great-grandmother of Israel's greatest king, David. If Boaz's mother was Rahab, would that go some distance in explaining his large-heartedness in marrying a Moabitess damsel, Ruth? Would he appreciate that since grace brought his mother into blessing, that he himself should show grace?

But as we travel down the list of names in Matthew 1, we find that the terminus is in the birth of "Jesus, Who is called Christ" (v 16). Matthew, guided by the Spirit of God, has included four women in his list, a most unusual addition in a Hebrew genealogy. Add to that that three if not all four were Gentiles, and then factor in that three of them had rather unsavoury biographies, and we see a foreshadowing of the truth which will end the gospel of Matthew: "Go ye therefore and teach all nations ..." (Matt 28:19). The gospel of Matthew may well have a Jewish audience in view, but it is a gospel for the nations, for the outcasts of society, and for the defiled and the defamed.

God in His own unique way thus has affirmed the choice made by Rahab by bringing her into the Davidic line and into the Messianic line. He takes a harlot under a curse, from the city of the curse, and elevates her to the honour of being linked with Israel's greatest King and with her Messiah. We are privileged to stand back and to observe the workings of amazing grace!

The New Testament Association

Rahab is mentioned in three portions in the New Testament (Matt

1:5; Heb 11:31; James 2:25). One interesting fact is that in each of these chapters, Abraham is also mentioned, James being the most obvious. She moves in the company with the nation's founder. God brings together the worst of the Gentiles, a harlot from Jericho, and the most esteemed of Israel's patriarchs, Abraham. God is displaying what grace can do, giving us a preview of the future when He would bring Jew and Gentile into a new thing, the Body of Christ.

In Matthew 1 to which we have referred, she is brought into the lineage of David and then the Messiah. In Hebrews 11, the stress is on her faith. In keeping with the theme of the chapter, she saw the future land of Canaan as belonging to the people of God, and she eagerly grasped the promise to her bosom. She wanted to be part of those people. An act that would be viewed as treason against her nation is heralded by God as an act of faith. This would hold special importance to believing Jews who were being accused of turning their backs against the nation and the promises made to the fathers.

In James 2, the stress is on her works. The same incident is mentioned, her receiving of the spies. Now, however, this act of treason is seen as visible proof of the reality of her faith. Abraham offering up his son and Rahab turning her back on her people – two acts totally contrary to reason, are presented as acts that justified them. Hebrews stresses that she received the spies; James that she sent them away a different way.

The structure of Hebrews 11 is also noteworthy. In verses 1-16, we have six men marked by faith and then a woman, Sarah. In verses 17-31 we have six examples of faith and a woman, Rahab. In the symmetrical structure, Sarah is paired with Rahab, another mark of divine favour and grace.

Our Education

As we review the story of Rahab together, a number of lessons strike me as being valuable to underline. If there was human wisdom involved in choosing the house of a harlot in which to find refuge, divine sovereignty was also at work in the choice. Rahab had believed the "report" she had heard of how God had brought Israel out of Egypt and dried up the Red Sea. She had long before recognised Jehovah as the true God and wanted to be linked with Him (Josh 10-11). Her "conversion" may well have been prior to the arrival of the spies. As a result, God sent the messengers to her door to give her more. God always supplies more light to those who move on the basis of the light He has given them. This provides an answer to all those who challenge believers with the question, "What about those who have never heard?" God is a just and merciful God.

We continually meet, on virtually every page of Holy Writ, reminders of the sovereignty and mercy of God. His character is revealed in incident after incident, shining like a many-faceted diamond for us to gaze upon and appreciate. It was not until Calvary that its full glory was seen.

While the placement of the books of the Bible is not divinely inspired, it was divinely controlled. I have often thought of the significance that Acts 28 is followed by Romans 1. In the former, Paul is seen gathering sticks and, in the process, is bitten by a snake. The people expect him to fall down dead, opining that he escaped justice in the sea and now must face it here at the fire. Here are a people who believe in a universe marked by moral government. To them God reveals not only moral government but matchless grace, as He sends a ship-wrecked evangelist to tell them of the gospel. In contrast, in the very next chapter (Romans 1), we have the record of those who reject light, deny moral order, and sink into deeper darkness.

Rahab's confession to the spies in Joshua 2:10-11 would also serve to "justify" God in His dealings with the nation. Thirty-eight years earlier they had turned back in unbelief. Yet Rahab here revealed that the hearts of the men of Jericho were fearful in light of the news which reached them of God's delivering power. The spies were fearful of the nations in the land of Canaan (Num 13, 14) and yet the truth is that the nations were standing in awe of God's mighty power and fearing for their lives. The generation that "turned back in the wilderness" was now gone, but the lesson would not be lost on the new generation of Israelites.

Rahab's confession would also confirm to the spies that God was going before them to prepare the way and ensure their victory. God was strengthening faith in His people, as well.

Another lesson is that grace received should result in grace shown. Boaz's mother, Rahab, had been a vessel of mercy. Grace had brought her into the nation and given her a place. She became the mother of Boaz who in turn displayed mercy and kindness to another "outsider," Ruth the Moabitess. We need fresh reminders that we who have been objects of divine mercy should be marked by mercy. We who have known forgiveness should be ready to forgive (Eph 4:32). As sons of the kingdom, we are expected to reflect the heart of our Father to the society around us (Matt 5:1-12, 48).

Finally, when she bound the line of scarlet in the window[1], she was turning her back on Jericho and looking for the coming of her deliverers. She was saying "goodbye" to the Jericho world and "hello" to the Israelite world. Her outlook was changed as well as her future.

[1]Consider windows in Scripture and events linked with them: David escaping through a window, Michal looking out at David, Paul escaping through a window; Eutychus and the window, Noah and the window in the ark; Daniel opening his window to pray.

Simeon

"Blessed are they that dwell in thy house:
they will be still praising thee. Selah"

Psalm 84:4

Reading: *Luke 2:25-35*

Throughout his gospel, Luke brings individuals together in pairs, at times for the purpose of contrast and at other times to reinforce a truth or principle. For example, Zacharias and Mary, Zacharias and Elisabeth, Elisabeth and Mary, Joseph and Mary, Simeon and Anna, the two debtors in ch 7 and the two sons Luke 15. There is the Rich Man and Lazarus in chapter 16, and the Publican and Pharisee of chapter 18. Two thieves on the cross, two angels at the tomb, and two on the road to Emmaus complete the picture.

In Luke 2, we are shown the portrait of two individuals, Simeon and Anna, a Man Ready to Leave and a Woman Waiting for Him to Come.

His Preparation

The Spirit of God is very prominent in the verses telling of the end of his days. Yet the tense of the verb suggests that this was the tenor of the man's life. He was just and devout – the work of the Spirit of God in a man's life, transforming his character. He was just toward men and devout toward God. The stress in his life is on character, not his gift or social standing. He was waiting to see the Lord's Christ. We learn about the atmosphere in which he lived (Spirit upon him), the announcement made to him (by the Spirit), the activity which marked him (in the Spirit).

It had been revealed to him from heaven that he would not see death before he had seen the Lord's Christ. Today, the Spirit teaches through the Word of God. Age is not a barrier to learning more of Christ. We must avoid a "past tense" Christianity. Consider Jacob on his deathbed and the fresh revelations he enjoyed. He spoke for the first time in Scripture of the Stone, Shepherd, Shiloh, and thy Salvation.

I learn that the work of the Spirit of God is in transformation of my character, anticipation of the coming Christ, and Revelation through the Word of God. His great desires are seen operative in the life of Simeon, but available to each of us. Am I willing to have the Spirit work in my life? Am I yielded? Do I have a desire to learn more of the Lord Jesus Christ?

His Location

Simeon is a just man. Those who move in House of God environs must be just men, those whose lives are consistent with the presence of God. As we see him enter the temple, we see God's perfect timing. Mary came with the type (the turtledove or pigeons) and the antitype (Christ) in her arms, and at that very moment Simeon came in as well. The Spirit of God is able to lead into the temple at the right moment. We have a man in the right place at the right time. David came to the battle just when Goliath was coming out boasting of his strength. Ruth came into the field at the same time as Boaz came from Bethlehem. Rebekah "happened" to arrive at the well just as the servant finished his prayer for guidance. God is able to bring each of us to the place and work He has designed for us. His timing is always perfect.

He came "in" *(en)* the Spirit into the temple. Did he expect the "Lord's Christ" to be a babe brought to the temple? We find that the Spirit brings men occupied with Christ into "House of God" conditions.

(There are 14 temple scenes in Luke worthy of your consideration.)

His Anticipation

Mary came bringing Christ in her arms. Simeon came expecting to see Christ. A person coming to the House of God to find Christ should never be disappointed. Mary came bringing Christ and Simeon came expecting Christ. If this were the norm for all our gatherings, we would have meetings that are truly honouring to the Lord and a rich blessing to us.

That places a burden of responsibility on all who handle the Word of God. While discussing verb tenses and the original meaning of words can enlighten as to the exegesis of a passage, we must always remember that believers need food for the soul as we gather in our Bible Readings and Ministry Meetings. Every believer should be able to leave with something from the Word of God that they can enjoy.

A Differentiation

The O. T. tells of men who wanted to die: Moses from discouragement, Elijah from depression, Job from destitution, and Jonah from his displeasure with God. All wanted to get away from something. In the N. T. there are two men who are ready to go home to heaven: Simeon because he could ask for nothing greater in life than seeing Christ, and Paul because he could think of nothing better than being with Christ.

"Master ... Thy servant ... you are allowing me to depart in peace." We have a soldier leaving his post of duty. Here is a man dying without regrets. He has fulfilled his course; he has had his heart's desire fulfilled. To live and then leave earth in this manner is something to be coveted by each of us.

The Revelation

Simeon is owned as a just man. In Luke 24, Joseph is called a just man. Both took the Lord in their arms: Simeon the baby and Joseph the body. To be able to "handle" Christ is a great honour but also a great responsibility. It is a delight to hear men rise on a Lord's Day and figuratively, take Christ in their arms and present Him to the Father. Simeon, Spirit led, is able to handle Christ in such a way that his praise ascended to heaven and Joseph and Mary were blessed.

"Thy salvation ... Thou prepared ... all peoples ... light to the Gentiles who are in darkness, and the glory of Thy people Israel." Christ is seen as the glory of the nation yet will know the greatest shame and reproach. His being spoken of as the glory of the nation corresponds to Paul's list of Israel's blessings in Romans 9:4, 5.

God has been slowly and compassionately revealing truth to Mary. The Song of Elisabeth, the visit of the shepherds, possibly the Magi and their gifts, all revealed some aspect of the Son that had been born to her. Now Simeon's song of praise adds to that revelation. Here she finds that He will be the Light to Gentile nations and the Glory of the nation of Israel. But Simeon adds one additional truth, a truth thus far hidden from this young mother. Sorrow lies ahead for her, the sorrow she will know at the cross. It was kind of God to give Mary six weeks of joy, unmingled by the shadows of the future. But Simeon's song of worship included that fact that a sword would pierce her. While on the one hand, these words must have caused her some measure of sorrow, yet when she stood at the cross, the awareness that all had been known to God at His birth would provide some measure of comfort.

Simeon's words were a revelation of Salvation, of coming Glorification, and of Preparation for her sorrow.

Appreciation

The Extent of the Blessing

The less is always blessed by the greater. Note that he does not "bless" the child in that sense. We do bless God when we speak of His greatness and exalted position. But that is not the same as us being a blessing to our brothers and sisters in Christ.

The Expectation for His Life

"The fall and rising of many … a sign spoken against." Simeon gave a brief summary of the life of the Lord Jesus in his prophetic-praise. He appreciated that this Babe was the focal point for the nation, the nations, and for eternity.

The Exposure of All Hearts

"Reasoning of many hearts revealed." Luke will now recount the exposure of man's thoughts about Christ as He moves among them. But more than that, Luke will be revealing the heart of the Friend of publicans and sinners in his gospel.

The Expanse of His Thoughts

Simeon is the N. T. Jacob, giving revelations of Christ at the end of his life: Saviour, Stumbling Stone, Sign, Sovereign, Sunlight, and Sword. His appreciation of Christ is global and cosmic. Anna's appreciation only a few verses later is more personal as the widow needed a kinsman redeemer.

The Implications

Mary came bringing a sacrifice for purification. Before she is able to bring her offering, she is interrupted by the entrance of Simeon who takes the child in his arms and utters his song of praise. This song of praise serves to banish any thought that the child needed a sacrifice. He is Himself the salvation and glory. The Spirit of God employed Simeon to jealously guard the holiness of the Son of God.

The Little Maid

"God is looking for those with whom He can do the impossible - what a pity that we plan only the things that we can do by ourselves."

A. W. Tozer

Reading: *2 Kings 5:1-19*

Her Situation – Captivity – Fate

It was not her fault. The spiritual tone in the nation of Israel was at a low ebb. Through the unwise decision of Rehoboam and the sovereign dealings of God, the nation had split into northern and southern kingdoms. The spiritual decline of the northern kingdom, Israel or Ephraim, was precipitous under the hand of Jeroboam. No ensuing monarch fared much better. The current king was marked by apostasy, and humanly appointed priests were functioning at Bethel and Dan, worshiping golden calves. God in His sovereign mercy had sent raiding parties into Israel to chasten and hopefully, to awaken consciences. As a result a little girl was taken captive and brought to Syria, there to serve as a slave to the wife of one of the great generals of the Syrian army.

The conditions in the nation were not her fault. Why did the hastening hand of God result in her captivity? What had she done? Why didn't the Syrians take the king or the priests or the men in power in the nation? Why set sights on a young girl such as she? Highly likely from the character of her witness, she would have been one of the faithful still left in the land of Israel. If anyone should have been spared, she would have been near the top of the list. She was suffering the governmental dealings of God because of the failure of others.

Her Spiritual Attitude – Her Faithfulness

What would your attitude have been if you were in her circumstances? Would you begin to question God? Question His wisdom? His justice? His sense of fairness? Did He even know about her or care? These, and a myriad of other doubts would assail the mind of most of us. We are not privy to whether she went through a stage when all these did attack her mind. We do not know if there was an initial stage of bitterness or struggle through which she passed. What we do know is that when we encounter her in 2 Kings 5, she is marked by a spiritual response to her trial. Rather than looking for a way out of the circumstances God had allowed, she looked to see how God could use her in her circumstances.

As the curtain opens on the scene in Syria, we find a young girl who is not marked by bitterness of rancor. There is no hint of self-pity or thoughts of anger in her heart. Rather than spite toward her captor, she displays faithfulness in her witness.

How do we view the seeming incongruities in God's dealings with us? Do we become bitter? Do we question God's wisdom? Or do we, as this young maiden, recognise the sovereign wisdom of God and seek to use our circumstances to serve Him? It may well be that she was taken away so as not to be part of a wicked nation (Isa 57:1). The recurring lesson of Scripture teaches the prosperity of those who bow to God's hand in their circumstances, not question His sovereign dealings in their lives. The story of Daniel and his three companions illustrates this beautifully.

The Lord Jesus underlined the remarkable nature of her faith. In Luke 4 in the synagogue at Capernaum, the Lord noted that though there were many lepers in Israel in the days of Elisha, none was cleansed but Namaan. No one in the nation had ever seen a person with leprosy cleansed. No one in the nation had the faith to come to the prophet and ask for cleansing. Yet, here was a slave girl away in Syria who believed that there was power present with the prophet in Samaria that could cleanse the leper.

Her Sympathy and Kindness – Her Features

Remarkably, she is marked by sympathy and kindness, courage, and confidence, as she addresses her slave master's wife. "Would God my lord were with the prophet that is in Samaria ...." (2 Kings 5:3). Note her respect – "my lord" – and her concern. Rather than wishing him ill, she is concerned for her captor's welfare. She is an Old Testament precursor of those who should be marked by the teaching of Matthew 5:44, "But I say unto you, Love your enemies, bless them that curse you, do good to them that hate you, and pray for them which despitefully use you, and persecute you." She was centuries ahead in her time, but right on time as to her character.

How do we respond to those who try to use us or manipulate us? Do we take character from our Father in heaven Who sends His rain upon the just and the unjust, and Who causes His sun to shine on men who blaspheme His name? The standard raised by the Lord Jesus in the Sermon on the Mount cannot be abrogated to Tribulation or Millennial saints. If we would be "perfect" as our Father is perfect, then, though the bar has been raised extremely high, this is what ought to mark us.

He Spiritual Fruitfulness

Testimony to Naaman

The faithfulness of the little maid led to Naaman's cleansing. But it did not stop there. In Old Testament language, it resulted in his conversion to the true God. His confession "Now I know that there is no God in all the earth but in Israel," (2 Kings 5:15) is his confession of faith. Also, his determination to only offer to the true God (v 18) is an indication of his change of heart.

The kindness of a little maid brought about the conversion of one of Israel's enemies. A Gentile bowed the knee to the God of Israel. Nothing more is said of Namaan, but we will meet him in heaven because of the faithfulness of a captive maid from the land of Israel.

Testimony to the King of Israel

When Namaan came with his gifts and entourage to the king of Israel, the king's unbelief and darkness were revealed in his response to Namaan. In his anger and frustration, with clothes rent and blood pressure rising, he did not even think of the possibility that God had a prophet in the nation who could heal the leper. Elisha, hearing of the arrival of Namaan, sent for him and the rest, as they say, is history. The unbelieving king was given a lesson that should have enabled him to know the true God. There is nothing in his history to suggest that there was even the slightest acknowledgment of the Lord. Yet God did not leave him without witness.

Testimony to Generations to Come

At first reading, we might think that the blessing from the captive maid was known by Namaan alone. Yet think for a moment of the myriads who have either come to understand the simplicity of salvation or received light from the story of Namaan. I often think that there will be a lengthy line of people in heaven, lining up to thank a rather insignificant Jewish maid, that she ever spoke up and expressed her conviction to Mrs. Namaan. Many will owe their conversion to Christ from this story.

Here is a fresh reminder that deeds done in faithfulness to the Lord will have ramifications far beyond what is originally intended by the doer. Your small acts of kindness, the tract you gave, the word of encouragement, the testimony you shared – all will arrive like waves on heaven's shore carrying with them results unexpected and surprising. Do not wait to do the "big thing," and let the myriad of minor deeds pass by you undone.

The Malefactor

"I had won Wimbledon twice, I was rich ... I had all the material possessions I needed. It is the old song of movie stars and pop stars who commit suicide. They had everything yet they are so unhappy. I had no inner peace."

Boris Becker

Reading: *Luke 23:32-43*

The story of the repentant thief of Luke 23 has been the basis for many gospel messages. Here is a man confronting death, yet alongside him is the Prince of Life. Feeling the emptiness of his life and the lack of peace, in a last-minute turn around in his attitude, he appealed to the Lord Jesus and is assured of a place in Paradise with the Lord Jesus. While not literally a death-bed conversion, it certainly is a last minute conversion. The points the gospel preacher can make and the lessons the sinner can learn are several: it is never too late to trust Christ. No sinner is too big a sinner to be saved. And salvation is not of works, baptism, or church attendance. It is simply by faith in the Lord Jesus Christ. Here is a man in heaven who has never participated in a debate between Calvinism and Arminianism, or free will and sovereign election. All he knew is that the Lord had said, "Today .. with Me...in Paradise."

I would, however, like to look at this incident through a different lens. There is material here for the saint to appreciate as well as devotional material that should stir us to worship and to wonder at the ways of God. Perhaps the best way to approach it is to consider:

What Christ Did for the Thief

Christ saved a thief. That is the most obvious truth from the story. Men shamelessly afforded Christ the centre place on skull hill that day, perhaps to imply that He was the most heinous of the three. The Lord used it to be near both thieves; to give an opportunity for each of them to receive salvation. One continued in his blasphemy; one repented and came to the Saviour for mercy. Salvation and mercy were available from this Saviour at the darkest hour. A man rejected and cast out by society, was going to be welcomed that day into paradise. A man who was associated with those who had committed murder and insurrection, was going to be accompanied by the Lord Jesus as he stepped into Paradise.

Imagination can be a liability, but you cannot help but wonder if this thief, obviously a Jew (unlikely for a Roman to be crucified), had attended the equivalent of Sunday School and learned truth about the coming Messiah. Where had he learned about a coming kingdom? What made him think that mercy was available for him? Was he thinking about the oft repeated statement in the Old Testament, "The mercy of the Lord endureth forever?"

Was there somewhere a pious Jewish mother weeping over the tragedy of her son's misdirected life. Was she there observing the events at Golgotha? Were her prayers answered at the last minute of his life? All this is a possibility, although we are not given insights into it.

Did the thief at that moment in time suddenly put together the teaching he had heard as a child? While all conversions are the work of the Spirit of God, truth learned in youth can be the soil which the Spirit uses to bring forth the fruit of conversion.

Once again we are reminded of a sovereign and good God. In His overruling care for men, He "arranged" for this thief to have one final opportunity of salvation. He had him crucified on the same day and on the same hill as His Son. The One Who came to seek and to save the lost would save one more lost soul in His final moments prior to His death.

What the Thief (and God) Did for Christ

Our thoughts normally centre on what the thief received from Christ. But there is another aspect to consider. Think of what the thief, and in actuality, God, did for the Lord Jesus. Just take apart the confession which the thief made and consider its implications.

"Lord," a confession of His person. "Remember me," a confession of His ability despite being impaled to a cross. "When You come in Your kingdom." The thief must have seen not only the value of the death of the Lord Jesus, but His resurrection, ascension, and coming kingdom. Despite what seems like the "end" for Christ, he saw Him returning to establish His kingdom. If so this was the greatest confession made to the Lord Jesus during His life on earth. The Father kept this for the last moments to encourage and strengthen His Son. How like a tender Father!

God strengthens the life of faith. He constrained six individuals, some of the most unlikely, to own the innocence and perfection of Christ. Both Pilate and Herod admitted they could find no cause of death in Him. Pilate's wife and Judas both owned Him as innocent. The Centurion spoke of Him as a "righteous Man," and the thief owned that He had done "nothing amiss." In this wonderful way, God sought to encourage the faith of His Son.

His confession would have thrilled the heart of the Lord Jesus. But an added joy was that He was able to save a soul on the brink of eternity. The mocking crowd threw in the face of the Saviour that He had saved others but Himself He could not save. What was the Saviour's response? He saved another and would not save Himself! Recall, as well, that it is Luke who tells us in chapter 15 about a shepherd Who seeks a lost sheep and, having found it, places it on His shoulders carrying it home, rejoicing. Isn't that the picture here? The Lord finds a lost sheep and places him on His shoulders, and takes him home to paradise, rejoicing. The Father provided this joy for His Son at the darkest hour!

Think as well of the contrast between the cries surrounding the cross and the confession of the thief. They were mocking His claim to be king. How could a King hang suspended on a Roman cross? Yet a thief recognises that here is a King Who is going to return and establish His kingdom, despite the cross and the nails. They were mocking His ability to save. To human eyes, the Lord Jesus was the epitome of weakness and helplessness. He could do nothing for Himself, much less do something for someone else. Yet the thief owned that this Man could save as he asked to be remembered in mercy in a coming day. The nation mocked Him as being the greatest transgressor, affording Him the centre cross. The charges of being perverter of the people, a blasphemer, an impostor, still filled the air. But the thief owned that He had done nothing amiss.

Finally, they were blaspheming His claim to be the Son of God. Though the thief did not use this specific language, he was owning the righteousness of all His claims when he looked ahead to a coming kingdom.

Bear in mind that in Luke's gospel, we are being afforded a view of a dependent Man Who is giving to God all that He ever sought to find in Man. God strengthens faith even in His Son Who was the author and finisher (perfect example, file leader) of faith. The confession of the thief would be a reminder (on the human level) of a coming kingdom for His Son. To see the future as bright as the promises of God at the darkest hour must have brought joy to the Saviour's heart.

Do continue to preach the gospel from this illustration. But also enjoy the insight into the heart of God and His care for His Son. Appreciate and worship at the vindication a thief afforded to the Lord at Calvary. Think finally, of the joy in the Shepherd's heart as He carried another sheep home rejoicing!

The Unnamed Servant

"Paul was overwhelmed at the divine presence and had no option but to lay himself unreservedly at the Lord's disposal."

Fred Stallan

Reading: *Genesis 24*

When we read Genesis 24, we have become so preconditioned to view it as a picture of the Spirit of God wooing and wining a Bride for the Master's Son, that we may actually, deprive ourselves of valuable lessons in servanthood. There is no question that after the altar experience of Genesis 22, the desire of a father for his son prefigures for us the work of the Spirit in our present age. On the literal level, the servant was a real man charged with a responsibility which he executed successfully. Add to that truth that every servant in Scripture should remind us of the Perfect Servant, either by way of contrast or similarity. So, there is much that we can glean from this servant's life and labour.

His Availability

It may appear to be a minor point, but when Abraham needed a servant for a very special work, this unnamed servant was available. If the Lord should burden you with a ministry, are you available? Our lives are "busy" by our own design. If we are too busy for God, we are busier than he ever intended us to be. This unnamed servant was available and ready for his master's call. Isaiah's "Here am I, send me" should be the ready response of each of us to any service with which the Lord entrusts us.

His Anonymity

We assume, and we may be correct, that the servant of Genesis 24 is "this Eliezer" mentioned earlier in Genesis (ch 15). That may be so. But it is significant that no name is mentioned in our chapter. He is one of the many nameless servants of Scripture. He joins a long list of men who are never named in Scripture, but who were raised up to deliver a message or perform a task, and then fade from the scene. Though unknown to us, they are known to God and will be honoured by Him. A lesson worth relearning is that God can pick up some of the seemingly most insignificant believers to accomplish His purposes.

We have a penchant for names and for those who have been successful in their ministry. We tend to think that God is dependent on men and machinery. God needs at times to jolt us back to the reality that He really does not need anyone of us. He managed to create the universe without my input and has successfully kept it going long before I came on the scene.

We hear of the homecall of a missionary, an evangelist, teacher, or elder and we wonder how the work of God will be sustained. While we value such men and women, we must remember that God's work does not rest on the shoulders of any one man, assembly, or mission field. God is able to provide replacements from some of the most obscure and unlikely places. Who ever heard of Elijah prior to 1 Kings 17 when he suddenly bursts upon the scene?

His Reliability

The task assigned to this servant was no small undertaking. Remember that in securing a bride for Isaac, Abraham is seeking to ensure the continuation of the line to which the covenant blessings have been made. Isaac needs a wife and offspring for the covenant to continue. I realise that God will not fail in regard to the covenant. But human responsibility is also at work in Genesis 24.

A monumental task such as this cannot be entrusted to a servant who is not reliable. How would God assess my reliability? There is a servant mentioned in 1 Kings 13 who delivered his message but failed to fully obey the Lord. You may well argue that the young man out of Judah was deceived by the old prophet, and he was. But faithfulness to the commission is a mark of reliability.

Paul gathered around himself two men who were of totally different temperaments but equally reliable: Timothy and Titus. He could entrust them with missions ranging from correcting an assembly, appointing elders, stirring up saints concerning a collection, and a host of others. Their ministry was carried out effectively and in accordance with the guidelines set down by the apostle.

In every assembly of the Lord's people, there are a myriad of tasks, some small and others more difficult, some public and many private, which need to be done. The responsible brethren normally look for those who are reliable to carry out those assignments. Strive to be reliable in your service for God.

His Capability

In His Search

We are all familiar with the story and the manner in which the servant sought the guidance of God in his quest. The first thing to underline is his dependence on God for the task assigned to him. He does not depend on his negotiating skills or the gifts he carries. He is looking to God for guidance.

And what of the sign for which he prays? Was it merely a matter of making it so hard to fulfil that if a damsel fulfilled it, then she must be the one? Or was something else in his mind?

Could I suggest that the sign requested reveals the wisdom and the divine guidance afforded the servant. He asks that the damsel who comes to the well and offers to not only provide him with water, but the camels as well, might be the one for his master's son. Now there were ten camels who had travelled a long way and needed a fill-up. Mr. Google informs me that a thirsty camel can drink up to 30 gallons of water at one time. Ten camels times 30 gallons comes to a staggering amount of water. That would mean refilling a pitcher many times and returning to the well repeatedly to meet the need. Here was a woman who was not afraid of work. Then the servant inquired about availability in her home. Notice the character traits he was exposing. He was seeking to determine if she was willing to work hard, was she hospitable, and was she considerate and kind? She may well have been attractive, but he was interested in the kind of woman he was going to bring back as a bride for Isaac.

Rebekah passed the first phase of the test. But there was another crucial matter to be addressed – the word of the master. The woman had to be of Abraham's kindred (Gen 24:4). He did not relate his message until he was sure of the lineage of the woman. There is a lesson here which needs to be stressed. The servant had requested a sign, a most unusual one, and one not easily fulfilled. Yet had the damsel been of the Canaanite tribes, I have no doubt the servant would have thanked her for the water, paid her handsomely, and moved on to another well. What is the lesson? The word of his master was more important than the fulfilling of a sign. The Lord may use signs at times to guide us. But if they are contrary to the Word of God, however promising the sign may appear, we can be sure the sign is not from God.

In His Dealings

Events now move to the house and the servant's interaction with Laban and Bethuel. The first thing we see is the priority which the master's commission had. Its take precedence over the meal that was set before him (v 33). His master's business would not take second place to even the necessities of life. Also, when they attempt to hinder his departure by the typical eastern customs of hospitality (see Judges 19, for example), he will allow nothing to hinder his completion of his task. He is a man totally committed to fulfilling the service given to him. He is a faithful steward.

The Lord Jesus in the gospels spoke of the necessity of prioritising the service of God. Necessities of life, natural relationships, and even self were not to hinder the servant of God in his devotion. What place does the service of God have in my life? Am I allowing the urgent to displace the important? We live in a society which imposes a sense of urgency upon us – mobile phones ringing, texts that must be answered ASAP, emails demanding immediate responses. All of these "urgent" things crowd out the important issue of a daily surrender of my life to the will of God. The servant of Genesis 24 had a single eye for the honour of his master.

Similar injunctions and exhortations are found in the epistles, all urging us to have a life marked by priorities and not subject to the demands of others, the call of a materialistic society, or the detours we allow in life.

In His Leading

The story nears its conclusion as we read that the woman followed the man, and that the servant took Rebekah and went his way. He was able to lead her to the master's son. Here was a man fit to follow. Can others follow my life, and will it lead them to the master's son? Is my service such that it brings men to a deeper appreciation of the Son? No doubt as the servant and Rebekah crossed the long distance back to Canaan, he would fill her mind with information about the man she had never seen but to whom she would soon be united. He knew the master and his son; he was able to fill her heart with truth that would increase her expectations and longings.

It is of interest that when Rebekah sees a man walking in the field (v 64) and inquires as to his identity, the servant does not identify him as his master's son. He said, "It is my master" (v 65). The day of espousal became the day when Isaac moved into the role of the master, the one who would continue the covenant.

In the Discharge of His Responsibility

"The servant told Isaac (not Abraham) all things that he had done" (v 66). His service ended with a day of accountability. Every servant must recognise that he is a steward and will be held accountable both for his service and faithfulness (1 Cor 4:2). Serving in light of a day of review is a solemn and searching balance to our labour. It will not only determine the honour we bring to Him, but also our usefulness in His eternal kingdom. May we be able to serve as did this nameless servant, with skill and selfless devotion.

Titus

"The Measure of a Man's greatness is not the number of servants he has, but the number of people he serves"

Selected

Reading: *2 Corinthians 7:5-16; 8:16-24; 12:17-18*

I might well be questioned for inserting Titus into this group of lesser lights. After all, he does have an entire epistle dedicated to him. He is mentioned nine times in 2 Corinthians and four additional times elsewhere. How can he be viewed as "minor"? In addition, if we measure a man by the quotation which heads this article, we will discover that Titus who served many men and many assemblies, was indeed a man marked by greatness. A minor man who was also great?

So, I must beg the reader's indulgence if I slip one or two "less minor" lives into this work. But in an attempt to justify his inclusion, may I ask you this? When was the last time you read an article or heard a message devoted to the man Titus, not the epistle which bears his name? He is often overlooked in favour of his more retiring fellow servant, Timothy. While both men served important roles under Paul, Titus does not get the ink that Timothy has received down through the years. Allow, then, this brief review of his life to begin to adjust the balance.

As mentioned, Titus is mentioned about 13 times in the N. T. The majority of those occur in 2 Corinthians, a result of his ministry and involvement there. His name has been subject to several different interpretations, one of them being "nurse." If we accept that meaning, it turns out to be a very apt description of the man and his ministry.

His Availability

We know very little of Titus' background aside from the fact that he was a Gentile. Some think that he was a brother to Luke, ascribing the absence of his name in the Acts of the Apostles to family "humility". If we can make some inferences from Acts 14 and 15, it would seem that Titus was from the assembly in Antioch. There is not universal agreement about the events of Acts 15 being linked with Galatians 1 and 2, but it does appear that Titus was among the "certain other of them" (Acts 15:2), who accompanied Paul. He was likely saved during the previous visit which Paul had made to Antioch since Paul refers to him as "my own son" (Titus 1:4). If these inferences are correct, Titus made rapid progress in his spiritual life as we will notice by the responsibilities with which Paul entrusted him.

His Greek background was valuable to the apostle Paul when he brought him up to Jerusalem in Acts 15 (Gal 2), as a test case on the thorny but critical issue of circumcision.

But Titus showed himself a ready and able servant by his trips for Paul to Corinth, Crete, Dalmatia, and Macedonia. His temperament differed from Timothy. If we can infer from Paul's letter to Titus while at Crete, Titus does not seem to possess the same reticence of personality that Timothy did. He did not need as much encouragement from the apostle to carry out his work. He had very delicate tasks assigned and appeared to have carried them out to the apostle's satisfaction.

A life such as that of Titus challenges each of us. Am I available for God to use? Am I so busy with "life," that I am not useful? Has the urgent taken priority over the important? Are all the devices of mass distraction so occupying me that I fail to wait upon God to find how He can use me? God needs none of us. Yet in incredible grace, God desires to use us to work with Him in accomplishing His great work here on planet earth. Is there any higher honour than to be of use to the God of our salvation?

His Versatility

Along with the variety of places to which Titus was sent, there were a variety of issues with which he had to deal. He was able to handle men who needed restoration, to handle money with integrity, and to resolve misunderstandings. He was able to muzzle the false teachers (Titus 1) in Crete. He was obviously a man of maturity, integrity, and sensitivity. He could be entrusted with a monetary gift for the saints in Jerusalem; he could discern men of character for leadership; he could be entrusted to preach the gospel in Dalmatia.

Not everyone is a "renaissance" Christian who can handle a multitude of tasks. The stress is on faithfulness with whatever the Lord has placed into your hands. Few men can match Titus for the many and varied tasks that Paul assigned to him. Your responsibility and mine, as stewards of the grace of God (1 Pet 4:10), is to be faithful with what has been given us to do for the Lord. We are not called upon to imitate Titus nor to be intimidated by his ability. We are called upon to learn that God is looking for men and women whom He can use for His work.

His Dependability

He was trustworthy and could be depended upon to handle money with honesty and integrity. He could be trusted to deliver a very difficult letter, one written with tears (2 Cor 2:4) and upon whose reception and response the apostle waited with extreme anxiety. He was discerning enough to be able to be entrusted with the responsibility of appointing elders in the assemblies in Crete. These would be believers younger in the faith, and many of them had considerable "baggage" that they were bringing with them out of Cretan idolatry and society. He would also have the spiritual maturity to be able to muzzle the false teachers at Crete. Paul valued his son in the faith, viewing him as an extension of his own ministry.

His Capability

At Corinth

Piecing together 2 Corinthians 2:13 and 7:6-14, Titus was sent with the letter which we call 1 Corinthians. It was a letter of correction to an assembly that had a very elevated view of itself, its gift, and its ability. To come with a letter of correction of such severity would be a daunting task for any man. Titus was a faithful steward. He showed himself able to handle truth in a hostile and unpopular arena.

Titus would also be present at Corinth to "nurse" the restoration of the assembly. Here then, is a rare and valuable ability. The restoration of believers and restoration of assemblies is fraught with many barriers and layers of difficulty. Yet, Titus was able to be instrumental in the recovery of an assembly to the truth of God. While it does not appear that everyone bowed to the letter (2 Cor 12:19-21), it does appear that the majority had sorrowed unto repentance and bowed to the apostle's rebukes (2 Cor 7:8-11).

Titus also was sent back to Corinth to remind the believers of their intention to give help to the poor believers in Jerusalem (2 Cor 8:6, 16, 23). Paul did not have to urge Titus too strongly as God had already put into his heart to do this and produce this "grace" in the hearts of the Corinthian believers. Certainly, urging believers to give of their substance is a delicate task which requires a wise and gracious man, a man above the suspicions of the believers. Very likely, Titus being a Greek and appealing to Gentiles for funds for Jewish believers in Jerusalem, would have been more effective than had a Jewish believer made the appeal.

Paul, as well, was so convinced of Titus' integrity that he could remind the believers that Titus was not there to collect money for him, a clandestine way of Paul getting support from them (2 Cor 12:18). Paul had total confidence in Titus, his motives, and manner. Paul could refer to Titus in this context as "walking in the same steps." He was Paul's "partner and fellow-helper" (2 Cor 8:23). Paul's words are high praise for a young man.

Can others have confidence in me concerning the truth of God? Concerning the handling of funds? Can older brethren entrust you with delicate and important tasks on behalf of the assembly? Not everyone is a Titus, but all can seek to live a life which is consistent and marked by fidelity and integrity.

At Crete

Titus appeared to have a special ministry to Crete. It seems that on release from his initial imprisonment by Rome (Acts 28), Paul and Titus travelled to Crete. While there, Paul saw several assemblies planted. Titus was left there with specific instructions (as given in the epistle bearing his name), for the new assemblies on the island. Titus' task was formidable considering the background of the new converts. He was to select elders, silence the gainsayers, speak up about the truth, and to support good works. This was totally counter-cultural for the new believers. Only the grace of God that had brought salvation (Titus 2:11, 12) could affect such a change.

The task of delegating leadership responsibility headed the list. The welfare and future of the assemblies depended on leadership. So, in delegating this task to Titus, Paul was entrusting him with the future of the work in Crete. No small task!

Then there was the silencing or muzzling of unruly and vain talkers. The spiritual edification of the assembly was in the balance. Titus needed to address these men for the blessing of the saints. Confrontation is not easy.

He had to speak up and instruct various classes of believers in the assembly to fulfil their responsibilities to each other (Titus 2:1-6), and remind all of the need to be subject to the government of the nation. Their prior lives had been marked by "lying, lawlessness, and laziness" (1:12). Now they were to be very careful to be marked out as model citizens. Finally, in contrast to their former life, they were to support good works whenever possible.

His role at Crete was the maturing of the believers and the furtherance of their spiritual lives. Paul reminds us elsewhere in his many "one another" statements, that among our responsibilities toward each other, we are to edify one another (1 Thess 5:11). Each of us should examine our life and manner to see if we are truly building up or tearing down. Am I a blessing or a blight? Titus left the assemblies in Crete the better by his visit. I should endeavour to leave every assembly, even every believer the better for having known me.

To Paul

We may think that the apostle was above the fray and exempt from the emotions with which we struggle at times. True, his anxieties were not directed to the same issues with which we struggle, but he did know strain and stress. He knew the "care of all the churches" which came upon him daily (2 Cor 11:28). In an insightful paragraph, he discloses to the Corinthian assembly that his love for them and his concern over their recovery was so great, that when he came to Troas and there was an opportunity to preach the gospel, he could not rest until he heard from Titus. What was the response of the assembly in Corinth to the letter he had sent? He had to press on to Macedonia in hopes of meeting up with Titus. So great was his joy at the news that Titus brought him when they finally met in Macedonia (2 Cor 7:5-7), that he spoke of it as a great comfort and that he "rejoiced the more" (v 7).

Here was a young man able to give encouragement to an older man. Here was an older veteran worker willing to take encouragement from a younger man!

Titus must have been a comfort to Paul in many ways. Along with that journey to Crete after Paul's release from his first imprisonment in Rome, he wanted Titus to come to Nicopolis for the winter (Titus 3:12). He obviously enjoyed the company of the younger man. Such was the spiritual maturity and character of Titus that he was an encouragement and comfort to the aged apostle.

Each one of us should strive to emulate, better, rather to develop, the spiritual character of a Titus that we might be available for God to use, dependable in our service, and an encouragement to others.